THE TEAPOT DOME SCANDAL TRIAL

A Headline Court Case

Headline Court Cases

THE TEAPOT DOME SCANDAL TRIAL

A Headline Court Case

Jonathan L. Thorndike

Enslow Publishers, Inc.

40 Industrial Road	PO Box 38
Box 398	Aldershot
Berkeley Heights, NJ 07922	Hants GU12 6BP
USA	UK

http://www.enslow.com

Library of Congress Cataloging-in-Publication Data

Thorndike, Jonathan L., 1959–
    The Teapot Dome scandal trial : a headline court case / Jonathan L.
Thorndike.
        p. cm. – (Headline court cases)
    Includes bibliographical references and index.
        ISBN 0-7660-1484-3   7- 02   j 345, 73 (2)
        1. Trials (Bribery)—United States—Juvenile literature. 2. Teapot
Dome Scandal, 1921–1924—Juvenile literature. [1. Trials (Bribery)
Teapot Dome Scandal, 1921–1924.]
    I. Title. II. Series.
      KF224. T39 T49 2001
      345.73'02323—dc21

                                                                    00-012166

Printed in the United States of America

10 9 8 7 6 5 4 3 2 1

To Our Readers:
We have done our best to make sure all Internet addresses in this book were active and
appropriate when we went to press. However, the author and the publisher have no
control over and assume no liability for the material available on those Internet sites or on
other Web sites they may link to. Any comments or suggestions can be sent by e-mail to
comments@enslow.com or to the address on the back cover.

Photo Credits: American Heritage Center, University of Wyoming, pp. 30, 78; Center for
Southwest Research, General Library, University of New Mexico, pp. 10, 51, 59; © Corel
Corporation, pp. 105, 109; Courtesy Automobile Manufacturers Association, Inc.,
Dictionary of American Portraits, Dover Publications, Inc., © 1967, p. 25; Courtesy
Library of Congress, *Dictionary of American Portraits*, Dover Publications, Inc., © 1967,
pp. 17, 35; Courtesy of Prints and Photographs Division, Library of Congress, pp. 21, 26,
29, 56; Courtesy University of Wisconsin, pp. 62, 91; *Dictionary of American Portraits*,
Dover Publications, Inc., © 1967, p. 85; Photo no. 7 (VII) 65, Frank Linderman Collection,
K. Ross Toole Archives, The University of Montana-Missoula, p. 93; Photo no.
76-217, K. Ross Toole Archives, The University of Montana-Missoula, p. 46; Photo
no. 81-219, K. Ross Toole Archives, The University of Montana-Missoula, p. 74;
Photo no. 89-272, K. Ross Toole Archives, The University of Montana-Missoula, p. 66;
State Historical Society of Wisonsin, negative # WHi (X3) 12289, p. 33; State Historical
Society of Wisconsin, negative # WHi (D484) 12809, p. 11; State Historical Society of
Wisconsin, negative # WHi (X3) 21369, p. 15; State Historical Society of Wisconsin,
negative # WHi (X3) 48451, p. 49; State Historical Society of Wisconsin, negative # WHi
(X3) 52469, p. 23; State Historical Society of Wisconsin, negative # WHi (X3) 52470,
p. 8; Wind River Photography, pp. 3, 42.

Cover Photo: Wind River Photography

Contents

The Teapot Dome Scandal 1921–1931	
Important People Involved:	
Harry M. Daugherty	Attorney General of the United States
Edwin Denby	Secretary of the Navy
Edward L. Doheny	President of the Pan-American Petroleum Company
Albert B. Fall	Senator from New Mexico and Secretary of the Interior
Warren G. Harding	United States President, 1921 to 1923
Gifford Pinchot	Chief Forester in the United States Department of Agriculture
Harry F. Sinclair	President of the Mammoth Oil Company
Harry Slattery	Conservationist and lawyer

Acknowledgments

Scholarly research and writing is a challenge, especially when the writer is teaching full time. However, I have had much assistance in the writing of this book. The library staffs at Belmont University and Vanderbilt University in Nashville, Tennessee helped locate rare primary sources such as the transcripts of Senate hearings in the 1920s. The photographic archives of the American Heritage Center at the University of Wyoming, University of Wisconsin, the K. Ross Toole Archives at the University of Montana, the State Historical Society of Wisconsin, and the Center for Southwest Research at the University of New Mexico provided images of the people involved in Teapot Dome. Jim Gores made a long drive to get the cover photograph of the rock formation in Wyoming. Toma Kimbro in the Honors Program at Belmont University provided secretarial support. Wonderful editorial assistance and advice came from Erin Cline, scholar of philosophy and Alpha Chi President at Belmont, and Dr. Jeff Coker of the Belmont University History Department. Claudia Thorndike put up with the many late nights and library trips in a supportive and loving way. Tate and Libby took an interest in the research and writing of this book. To these people and unnamed others, I owe many thanks.

chapter one

THE MYSTERIOUS DEATH OF PRESIDENT HARDING

TRAGEDY—On August 3, 1923, the headline in *The New York Times* screamed in bold block letters: **"PRESIDENT HARDING DIES SUDDENLY . . . CALVIN COOLIDGE IS PRESIDENT."**[1] Warren Gamaliel Harding, the twenty-ninth president of the United States, was only fifty-nine years old when he died in a hotel in San Francisco, California. He was not, however, the first president to die while in office. Five others before Harding—William Henry Harrison, Zachary Taylor, Abraham Lincoln, James Garfield, and William McKinley—had also died in office.[2]

President Harding is generally remembered for the Teapot Dome Scandal. It was very complicated, and it took ten years, two congressional hearings, and many court cases to resolve. After Harding became president in 1921, Secretary of the Interior Albert B. Fall persuaded him to secretly transfer control of three huge government oil

Warren Harding (shown here) was not the first president to die while in office. Five others before Harding–William Henry Harrison, Zachary Taylor, Abraham Lincoln, James Garfield, and William McKinley–had also died while in office.

reserves from the Navy to the Department of the Interior. One of those oil reserves was ten thousand acres at Teapot Dome, Wyoming. The other two were at Elk Hills and Buena Vista in California. The secretary of the interior is supposed to work toward conserving and developing the nation's natural resources, but Fall secretly leased the government oil reserves to his friends, Harry F. Sinclair and Edward L. Doheny. Both owned oil companies. Fall got rich by leasing the oil fields to his friends. He received a great deal of money in the form of bribes from Sinclair and Doheny in exchange for the leases. Unfortunately, this was illegal and unethical. Fall stole government-owned property and sold it.

Once the scandal became public after Harding's death, a congressional committee led by Senator Thomas J. Walsh of Montana forced Albert B. Fall to resign. The Supreme Court of the United States cancelled the leases made to Sinclair and Doheny in 1927, and Fall and Doheny served time in jail. Harry F. Sinclair was cleared of all charges and never went to prison.

When President Harding died, he was trying to win a second term as president. He needed to win the nomination of the Republican party. So, he started a two-month trip he called "A Voyage of Understanding" in order to meet people, make speeches, and make a good impression on the American public.

In the 1920s, the railroad was the only option for traveling long distances. Regularly scheduled airplane travel was not yet common. In 1923, Harding left Washington, D.C.,

As secretary of the Interior, Albert B. Fall (shown here) persuaded President Harding to secretly transfer control of three huge government oil reserves from the Navy to the Department of the Interior.

with his wife and a party of sixty-five people including Secret Service agents, reporters, photographers, and technicians, for a train trip that would travel through many western states. The president planned to make many stops along the way to meet the people who lived there. The technicians would install amplifiers and long-distance telephone connections so that people all over the country could listen by radio to Harding's speeches.[3] The train was called *The Superb*, and it had ten cars with a luxurious hotel-like suite car at the end for President and Mrs. Harding.

As the train left Washington, D. C., on June 20, a Navy band played a joyful tune of farewell. No one knew that Harding would not live to return to Washington. Harding, however, did show signs of fatigue and mental weariness even before the train pulled out of the station. Presidential assistants said Harding was not resting or relaxing between meetings and speeches. He worried about his reputation and his chances of winning reelection. He knew he needed to make a strong impression during this trip so that people would vote for him.

The train stopped first in West Virginia, before making stops in many towns along the way out West. Harding stood on the rear platform of the train in his gray suit posing for photographs, making speeches, shaking hands, and greeting the public. He seemed friendly and cordial. The train glided through Ohio, Indiana, Illinois, and into the Midwest. President Harding insisted on appearing in public at every stop, but this exhausted him.

The sun and wind blistered his lips, and his personal physician put ice on his mouth to help him look and speak better. Harding noticed that the crowds who came to greet the train were not very large or responsive. This made him try even harder to make better speeches.[4]

In St. Louis, Missouri, Harding made a speech in front of ten thousand people at a convention. Harding's speech was about the need for the United States to participate in world affairs to avoid another catastrophe like World War I. But the audience did not like Harding's plea to have the country be more active in world affairs. People were more interested in managing their own lives. No one clapped after the speech ended.

After the death of Harding, a congressional committee led by Senator Thomas J. Walsh of Montana (shown here) forced Albert B. Fall to resign.

America had only reluctantly entered World War I in 1917. Many people did not want to get involved in world affairs so soon after the war.

For the first time, Americans were able to listen to a live broadcast of Harding's speeches on the radio. This, however, only added pressure to Harding to make sure his speeches were well done. The radio equipment made him nervous, and Harding did not make his normal speaking gestures. He was also growing very tired from the long trip. However, Harding was sincere in his desire to promote morality and responsibility. He said:

> I shall not restrict my appeal to your reason. I shall call upon your patriotism. I shall beseech your humanity. I shall invoke your Christianity. I shall reach to the very depths of your love for your fellow countrymen of whatever race or creed throughout the world. . . . My soul yearns for peace. My heart is anguished by the sufferings of war. My spirit is eager to serve. My passion is for justice over force.[5]

When the train left for Kansas City, Missouri, Harding's "lips were swollen and blue, his eyes puffed, and his hands seemed stiff."[6] Harding seemed to be depressed and plagued by worries. Harding told a reporter, "My God, this is a h[_ _ _] of a job! I have no trouble with my enemies . . . but my . . . friends . . . they're the ones that keep me walking the floor nights!"[7] Apparently, something weighed heavily on Harding's mind. Was he worried about the illegal activities of his Cabinet? Did he even know about them? Whatever the reason for his concerns, President Harding was not having a good trip.

In Denver, Colorado, Harding told an audience of twelve thousand people that the Eighteenth Amendment (prohibiting the sale, manufacture, or consumption of alcoholic beverages) would never be reversed. He demanded rigorous enforcement of the law (despite the fact that the Justice Department was not doing its job of making sure the law was followed).

In Salt Lake City, Utah, Harding departed from his written speech to talk about the country joining in on world affairs.[8] Harding's voice was low and sounded sad. He made no gestures with his hands during the speech. But for the first time, he enjoyed a rousing reception as the audience clapped loudly after the speech ended.

Harding got a much-needed break from the hectic speaking schedule with a visit to Zion National Park in Utah. He dedicated a branch of the Union Pacific Railroad near where connecting track had been laid in 1869, completing the East-West rail line at Promontory Point, Utah.[9]

From Salt Lake City, Harding traveled through Wyoming, Montana, Idaho, Oregon, and Washington State. In Washington, the president got on a boat for a one-thousand-mile sea voyage to Alaska. Traveling in Alaska, Harding thought the scenery was pleasant but not overly impressive. He preferred the flat regularity of his native Ohio to the splendor of mountains, glaciers, and the ocean.[10]

After returning from Alaska, Harding planned to make major speeches in Portland, Oregon; San Francisco, California; and Los Angeles, California; but he unexpectedly stumbled and almost fell on stage while speaking in Seattle. The trip was wearing him down. The audience in Seattle could see the exhaustion written on his face and the lack of color on his cheeks. Several times during his speech in Seattle, Harding hesitated and called Alaska "Nebraska" by mistake. Halfway through his speech, he stumbled, dropped the manuscript, and grabbed the podium in front of him. An alert aid, Herbert Hoover, picked up the pages that had fallen to the floor and handed them to the president.[11] Later, Harding's doctor, Charles E. Sawyer, said the incident was due to some bad seafood that Harding had eaten while coming back from Alaska. Dr. Sawyer also said that it was not serious and posed no threat to Harding.

On July 29, 1923, Harding got back on the train and went to San Francisco. He died there on August 2. On the evening of August 2, before he died, Harding propped himself up with pillows in bed as he listened to his wife read aloud "A Calm Review of a Calm Man," a flattering article about him published in the *Saturday Evening Post*. The author, Samuel Blythe, wrote that the president was following a steady course, carefully pursuing his goals without paying attention to the complaints of critics.[12] Many people across the country liked Harding. He was steady and predictable. He came from a small-town business background, so he was sympathetic to the needs of business people. He did not want to risk losing friends by taking sides or starting expensive new government programs.[13] Journalist William Allen White wrote that it would have been impossible for doctors to know what was wrong with

Many people all over the United States liked President Harding. He was known to be steady and predictable.

Harding: "How could the doctors diagnose an illness that was part terror, part shame, and part utter confusion!"[14]

The nation was amazed by the president's death, and Mrs. Harding was ordered to bed by the family physician.[15] Dr. Sawyer thought that a burst blood vessel in Harding's brain had caused his death. An autopsy, an examination of the body, would have provided valuable medical evidence. Mrs. Harding, however, would not allow an autopsy to be performed. She did not want to disturb her husband's dead body. President Harding might also have died from a massive heart attack, but that remains a mystery. Dr. Sawyer signed the death certificate without performing an autopsy.

Herbert Hoover, then secretary of commerce and a personal friend of President Harding's, was the first member of the Cabinet to reach the bedside of the dead president. Hoover rushed through the hallway. He was aware that Harding's life was quickly ending. He came out into the hallway of the hotel a short time later. He was completely overcome with emotion; tears ran down his cheeks and he could not speak to the reporters gathered outside. San Francisco mayor James Ralph was the next to arrive, and he also left without speaking. The grief and shock of Harding's friends and family were extreme.[16]

With President Harding dead, many questions had to be answered. Did Harding die of a "broken heart" because of the corruption associated with the Teapot Dome scandal? Could someone have poisoned Harding? Did a hit man connected with organized crime murder Harding because of the Eighteenth Amendment? People were surprised by

At the time of President Harding's death, Herbert Hoover (shown here) was secretary of commerce and a personal friend of the president.

Harding's death, so they passed along rumors in order to explain it. But none of these rumors was ever proven. We do know that Harding died of natural causes, but without an autopsy, the exact cause of death would never be known. A reporter for *The New York Times* wrote of Harding's death, "nothing could have been a more shocking surprise." The formal announcement released by the White House said:

> The President died at 7:30 P.M. Mrs. Harding and the two nurses . . . were in the room at the time. Mrs. Harding was reading to the President, when, utterly without warning, a slight shudder passed through his frame; he collapsed, and all recognized that the end had come. A stroke . . . was the cause of his death.[17]

Was President Harding responsible for the scandals that took place during his years in office? It is difficult to assign responsibility, but historians, lawyers, and government officials found plenty of evidence of wrongdoing. There was plenty of blame to go around, but nobody was willing to stand up and take it, and President Harding was dead. Government officials, Harding's Cabinet members, and business leaders involved in the scandals were afraid of being punished. What remained to be seen was what could be proven in Senate hearings and courtroom trials once the public heard about Teapot Dome.

chapter two

AMERICA IN THE JAZZ AGE

THE JAZZ AGE—What was America like in the 1920s? The United States had only forty-eight states. Alaska and Hawaii were not yet states. The country's population was lower than today's population and not as heavily concentrated in major cities like New York, Chicago, and Los Angeles. The population was 106 million, divided about equally between urban and rural areas. The average salary in 1920 was $1,236 per year, but the cost of living was much lower than it is today. At the grocery store, a loaf of bread cost twelve cents, a dozen eggs cost sixty-eight cents, and a quart of milk (which might be delivered by horse-drawn buggy or truck) cost seventeen cents.[1]

The Impact of World War I

The second decade of the twentieth century brought major political and economic changes in the United States and Europe that affected almost every American. America emerged as a new global power following World War I. This first global war using "modern" war technology became a bloody stalemate that cost the lives of almost 10 million soldiers in Europe. America's involvement in World War I helped create the mood of disillusionment that surrounded Teapot Dome.

During World War I, Germany expanded its military supremacy and attempted to conquer France. The Central Powers—Germany and Austria-Hungary—were aided by the Ottoman Empire (Turkey) and Bulgaria in heavy trench fighting and artillery bombardment. For four years, the Central Powers fought against the Allied Powers—Russia, France, Belgium England, Japan, Italy, and the United States.[2] The United States entered World War I relatively late, in April 1917. The United States thought about entering the war after a German submarine sank the British steamship *Lusitania* in 1915. The *Lusitania* was torpedoed without warning off the coast of Ireland, killing nearly 1,200 people aboard, including 128 Americans. Until the *Lusitania* sank, Americans supported President Woodrow Wilson's policy of neutrality (not wanting to get involved).[3]

President Wilson had been only two weeks into his second term in office in 1917 when he got word that three American ships had been sunk by German submarines. Politicians and military leaders argued that deliberately sinking ships was an act of war, but Wilson hesitated to get involved. On January 22, 1917, President Wilson gave his famous "Peace without Victory" speech to Congress. In the speech, he proposed a cooperative peace in Europe and a League of Nations that would prevent future wars.[4]

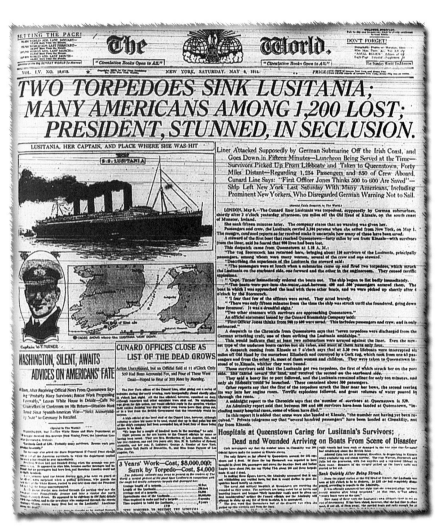

The New York World *announced the* Lusitania *disaster on the front page of its May 8, 1915, edition. Below the photograph of the* Lusitania, *a map pinpoints where the liner was sunk off the southern coast of Ireland.*

After Germany sank the American ships, President Wilson asked for the opinions of the members of his Cabinet. Even Secretary of the Navy Josephus Daniels, who had hesitated to get involved from the beginning, now saw no other option but to declare war. Wilson reluctantly signed the declaration of war on April 2, 1917. Wilson said, "We enter this war only where we are clearly forced into it because there are no other means of defending our rights."[5]

After the United States entered the war, British Prime Minister Lloyd George said America became "a world power in a sense [it] never was before."[6] People thought World War I was the "war to end all wars." People also thought it would make the world safe for democracy after the threat of military dictatorship by Germany and Austria-Hungary was eliminated.

President Wilson went to the Paris Peace Conference in 1919 to sign the Treaty of Versailles, officially ending military action against Germany. The French greeted him warmly as a savior of democratic values. The world now thought of the United States as a major participant in world affairs.

Surprisingly, disappointment followed Wilson's signing of the Treaty of Versailles. President Wilson had wanted to create a League of Nations that would prevent future conflicts, but, instead, France, England, and other European nations demanded severe financial repayment of war losses. Germany lost 13 percent of its land once the boundary lines in the treaty were drawn out.[7] John Maynard Keynes, a British economist, wrote that the terms of the treaty instilled

After the sinking of the Lusitania, *Secretary of the Navy Josephus Daniels (left) advised the president that the United States had no other option but to declare war.*

in Germany an overwhelming sense of injustice, that they were being unfairly punished. The Treaty of Versailles made German citizens yearn for a new leader who could drag them from out of the shadows of war. Germany would find a new leader in Adolf Hitler, who in 1933 was elected chancellor. Hitler soon started rebuilding the military and leading Germany into the global catastrophe of World War II, Nazism, and the Holocaust.

Americans, meanwhile, also withdrew from President Wilson's idea of a League of Nations. The United States faced serious internal problems after the war. There were work stoppages by powerful labor unions (workers' rights groups), increases in the cost of living, inflation, and the struggle to enforce the Eighteenth Amendment. The issues at home seemed too important to spend much time thinking about European politics. Americans turned away from the activism of President Theodore Roosevelt (1900–1908) and that of President Woodrow Wilson (1912–1920). After World War I, Americans wanted politicians who would decrease government activism, lower taxes, and avoid involvement with Europe.

President Wilson hoped that the League of Nations, created at the Paris Peace Conference in 1919, would resolve conflicts in Europe. However, Congress failed to ratify the United States's entry into the league.

The Lifestyle of the 1920s

America was in high gear during the 1920s. Industrial production increased tremendously. Citizens enjoyed a higher standard of living. Industrialist Henry Ford was producing automobiles and paying his workers more than ever before.[8] From 1921 to 1929, Americans enjoyed great wealth. As companies paid their workers more, people were able to spend money on luxuries like cars, movies, sporting events, cosmetics, jewelry, and entertainment. This period of prosperity ended on "Black Thursday," October 24, 1929, when the Wall Street stock market in New York started a tremendous downward plunge that marked the start of the Great Depression of the 1930s. The Depression was a worldwide business slump during which many people lost their jobs, and in many cases, everything they had worked so hard to earn in the 1920s.

The 1920s were a time of increased industrial production in the United States. Henry Ford was producing automobiles and paying his workers more than ever before.

Historians called the 1920s the Roaring Twenties, the Jazz Age, and the Age of Affluence because America seemed filled with boundless energy and wealth. The 1920s were a time of upward mobility and cultural creativity. Radio broadcasts gave everyone access to musical performances and comedy shows. Enrico Caruso, an Italian opera singer, and Al Jolson, a vaudeville theatrical star, became famous to millions through radio broadcasts. Musicians Louis Armstrong, Bessie Smith, and Fats Waller became household names during the Jazz Age. More movie theaters were built, so film stars like Rudolph Valentino, Mary Pickford, and Charlie Chaplin became celebrities better known than politicians.[9]

As companies expanded and hired more workers, more Americans were drawn to the cities in the North like Boston, Chicago, New York, and Philadelphia. People began driving cars instead of horse-drawn buggies for transportation. In 1920, approximately 8 million cars were on the road. In 1929, there were almost 23 million cars. All those new cars needed to run on gasoline made from oil that was at the center of the

By 1929, there were almost 23 million cars on the road in the United States. All of those cars needed to run on gasoline made from the oil that was at the center of the Teapot Dome scandal.

Teapot Dome scandal. Cities grew and became the busy urban centers that we recognize today. Larger cities provided shelter from enforcement of the Eighteenth Amendment. The Eighteenth Amendment made "the manufacture, sale, or transportation of intoxicating liquors" illegal.[10] The amendment was introduced by a long campaign of "progressives" and antialcohol groups called temperance societies. Unfortunately, this led to bootlegging (illegal manufacture of alcohol) and disregard for the law. Speakeasies (secret clubs where people bought alcohol) and the increase of organized crime activity, especially in Chicago, caused a strong public reaction. Speakeasies gave people back-alley restaurants or taverns to purchase illegal alcohol and do the Charleston, a popular dance. The Eighteenth Amendment was eventually reversed by the Twenty-First Amendment in 1933, which made the manufacture and sale of alcohol legal once again.[11]

New Freedoms

For young people, the 1920s were a time to rid themselves of the old ways of doing things. Women enjoyed more freedoms. They earned the right to vote and participate in the political process in 1920 as a result of the tireless campaigning of the "suffragists" (women who campaigned to pass the Nineteenth Amendment to the Constitution).[12] Women started attending college and pursuing careers. Flappers—young women who cut their hair short and wore less restrictive, revealing clothing—shocked some people.

They sometimes played sports, smoked, drank, and went to clubs formerly reserved for men only.[13]

Not all Americans liked the new freedoms. Many people resisted the idea of women voting, smoking, and wearing new hairstyles and clothing. For some, the 1920s seemed to usher in a lack of morals and traditional values. The two most famous court trials of the 1920s—the Sacco and Vanzetti trial and the Scopes "Monkey" trial—showed that many Americans would not tolerate new ideas.

In 1921, Nicola Sacco and Bartolomeo Vanzetti, immigrants from Italy, were convicted of murder and executed. Prosecutors at their trial emphasized the anti-American political beliefs and foreign birth of the accused men more than the facts of the case.[14]

In 1925, in Dayton, Tennessee, biology teacher John T. Scopes was put on trial for illegally teaching Charles Darwin's theory of evolution. Reporters named the case the "Monkey Trial," and journalist H. L. Mencken described it as a triumph of superstition over science.

Americans wrote books expressing the mood of the time. F. Scott Fitzgerald's *The Great Gatsby* portrayed the American dream of wealth and rising social status in an ironic light. Ernest Hemingway in *The Sun Also Rises* wrote of a "lost generation" of Americans who decided to live in Europe because they did not feel comfortable in America any more. William Faulkner described the moral decline of the American South in *The Sound and the Fury*. Sinclair Lewis satirized the shallowness of a midwestern real-estate broker in his novel *Babbitt*. In his epic poem of sorrow

Clarence Darrow, the lawyer who defended John Scopes during the Scopes "Monkey Trial" is shown here.

entitled *The Wasteland*, T. S. Eliot wrote about the loss of moral certainties in the modern world.

Harding's Rise to President

How did Warren G. Harding, a calm businessman from a small town in Ohio, get to be president during this turbulent decade? President Theodore Roosevelt had died in 1919, and there was no favorite candidate. The Republican nomination became a wide-open race crowded with unknown people. Three candidates quickly positioned themselves to gain the nomination: General Leonard Wood, Hiram D. Johnson, and Frank O. Lowden.

General Leonard Wood thought he was the favorite because he had commanded Roosevelt's "Rough Riders"

*General Leonard Wood (left) and President Warren G. Harding (right)
are shown here. General Wood was a war hero in the Spanish-American
War and a leading Republican candidate for president.*

military unit during the Spanish-American War in 1898.
Wood won a Medal of Honor for fighting the Apache tribal
leader Geronimo in Arizona, and he was a Harvard medical
school graduate. Wood's chances of winning the nomination
were hurt, however, by the news that he had spent $1.5
million on his campaign, most of it donated by one
businessman from Cincinnati, Ohio. The size of his
campaign budget made it seem as if Wood were trying to
buy the presidency. Voters did not like their candidates to
come from wealthy families, in part because Americans like
people who have worked hard to earn their wealth as rulers
of our country.

Governor Frank O. Lowden of Illinois also had the liability of having money. His wife's family owned the company that made Pullman railroad cars.

Senator Hiram D. Johnson of California entered the race as a "progressive" reformer.[15] A progressive reformer tries to use new ideas to change old political beliefs. A young Ohio politician and businessman named Warren G. Harding was the last candidate to enter the race.

At the Republican National Convention, the nominating committee had difficulty deciding who among all of the choices would be the best candidate to represent the Republicans. The candidates received votes in this order: Wood, Lowden, Johnson, and Harding. The future president came in last place on the first ballot. Ballot after ballot produced closer results, and eventually the four candidates received an almost equal numbers of votes.

What did Harding have that allowed him to win the nomination? He was handsome, easygoing, and he gave inspired speeches that did not upset anyone. He made no drastic claims of change for the future. Harding represented "normalcy," a comforting idea during a time when America had recently come through a war. Harding's humility and confidence impressed delegates. Adding to his appeal was the fact that Harding was from Ohio, a solid political base called "the mother of Presidents" because six of the last ten presidents had come from there.[16]

Harding also had business experience as a publisher and editor of newspapers, and important political experience. Harding had nominated President Taft in the 1912

Republican National Convention. In 1914, Ohio elected Warren G. Harding to the Senate, and he was promoted to keynote speaker of the 1916 Republican National Convention. After Roosevelt's death, newspapers widely discussed Harding as a possible nominee for president in 1920.

When Harding received the nomination of the Republican party, he gave an acceptance speech in Marion, Ohio. He said he was aware of the awesome responsibilities of president and of his own limitations, but faith in God and America would see him through. From then on, Harding promoted himself relentlessly, starting with his famous "front porch" campaign from his home. Many people came to Marion to listen to Harding speak. Politicians, reporters, farmers, factory workers, military veterans, religious people, and other citizens gathered around the front porch of the stately old mansion. Sometimes show business celebrities came to entertain the crowds. At the end of September, Harding hit the road and campaigned in ten states before the November election.

When the election arrived, people were ready to blame President Wilson for the higher cost of living, higher taxes, immigration problems, and entanglement in foreign affairs. People were bitter about the loss of American soldiers in World War I. Voters wanted a Republican in this election since President Wilson had been a Democrat. Democrats knew they were unpopular and likely to be unseated. President Wilson had suffered a stroke and could not run for reelection. The best hopes for the Democrats lay in three

When the election arrived, people were ready to blame President Wilson for the high cost of living, higher taxes, immigration problems, and entanglement in foreign affairs.

candidates: Attorney General A. Mitchell Palmer, Secretary of the Treasury William G. McAdoo, and Ohio governor James M. Cox.[17] The Democrats nominated Cox as their candidate.

Harding and Cox had similarities: both were newspaper publishers from Ohio, both were politically experienced, and both made wise choices for their running mates. Harding had chosen Massachusetts governor Calvin Coolidge as his vice presidential candidate, and Cox selected Assistant Secretary of the Navy Franklin D. Roosevelt. Both of these vice presidential candidates would go on to become presidents.[18]

During the campaign season, both Republicans and Democrats failed to deal with the most important issue of 1920: the Eighteenth Amendment, the prohibition on the manufacture and sale of alcohol. Both Harding and Cox campaigned on the issue of the League of Nations. Cox wanted the United States to join the League of Nations because Wilson had invented it. Harding opposed it.

Republican Approach

The Republicans had a strong political organization. They distributed a poster showing Harding standing beside a flagpole with the Stars and Stripes waving proudly overhead while Cox attempted to quickly raise the League of Nations flag. This image suggested that Harding would defend American freedoms while Cox would be held back by his responsibility to the League of Nations. When making a speech, Harding presented himself as dignified, likable, and

Democratic presidential candidate James Cox chose Assistant Secretary of the Navy Franklin D. Roosevelt (shown here) as his vice presidential candidate.

practical. Harding would not make impulsive changes: "[N]obody is going to make me lose my temper and indulge in impulsive utterances," he said in one speech.[19] He tried to be friendly to all types of people, including businesspeople, working people, union leaders, veterans, and progressives who felt the Democratic party had lost its way.

Democratic Approach

Meanwhile, Democrat James M. Cox tried to emphasize the League of Nations as the best hope for lasting peace in the world. Cox accused Republicans of trying to buy the election by spending so much money on their campaign. But people thought of Cox as Wilson's puppet. Many thought Cox was too liberal. Harding insisted that American membership in any world organization had to give the country the freedom to act in its own defense and decline to participate in any international military action.

Harding's Promises Get Him Elected

Warren Harding promised no new political programs but simply a "return to normalcy." Voters liked Harding's message, and Harding won thirty-seven out of forty-eight states, or 60 percent of the popular vote in the election. Democrat James M. Cox earned 34 percent of the vote, and Socialist candidate Eugene V. Debs was a distant third place with only 3 percent of the vote. The Republicans regained control of the government, and they wanted to reestablish their authority after eight years of President Wilson's leadership. Americans deeply wished to end their international involvement, and Harding was just the person to fill that wish with his "return to normalcy" theme.

After he was elected, Harding gave a speech to Congress stating in what direction he thought the country should go for the next four years. Harding's philosophy of government seemed to open the way for the Teapot Dome scandal. He said that Americans might regret our involvement in World War I, but now we must "undertake our work with high hope, and invite every factor of our citizenship to join in the effort to find our normal, onward way again."[20] Harding wanted to focus on important issues in the United States such as the federal budget.

Harding Favors Business Freedom and Growth

Harding also wanted American businesses to keep expanding. He wanted Americans to buy American-made products. So he called for an "instant tariff enactment," putting high taxes on goods brought into the United States from other countries. Harding also said he wanted to reduce the size of the federal government. The "high cost of living is inseparably linked with high cost of government," Harding said. He wanted to promote "less government in business as well as more business in government," a cutback on federal rules and supervision of American industry. Harding clearly supported free enterprise: "[T]here is no challenge to honest and lawful business success."[21]

So from the beginning, Harding meant to give business and industry freedom to do as they pleased. This was what the American people wanted in 1920. Industrial productivity and advancement would help the country recover from World War I.

It did not take long, however, for scandals to surface during Harding's presidency. Serious accusations against Harding and his Cabinet began in 1923, two years after he took office.

Many people thought the Department of Justice led by Attorney General Harry M. Daugherty was covering up illegal activities such as selling alcohol or profiting from not enforcing other laws. Daugherty was at the bottom of the rumors, so many lawmakers tried to force him to resign. On December 1, 1922, Representative Oscar Keller of Minnesota filed fourteen charges of impeachment against the attorney general.[22] Impeachment is a process in which lawmakers can accuse a government official of wrongdoing while in office and bring the complaint to trial.

Keller's suit claimed that Daugherty did not enforce existing antitrust laws. Antitrust laws were passed in order to prevent big businesses from creating monopolies. A monopoly happens when a single company totally dominates the market and puts other companies out of business. Keller could not produce specific evidence of illegal activity, however. In January 1923, the judiciary committee voted to dismiss the allegations.

President Harding thought Keller held a personal grudge against Daugherty.[23] Yet, Keller's charges were just the beginning. Soon, a sea of troubles leading to Teapot Dome would surround President Harding and his White House staff. At first, citizens and politicians went about their business and did not think much of the rumors. As evidence began to build, however, a real scandal began to grow beneath the gossip.

Scandals Uncovered

The first major scandal of the Harding administration involved Charles R. Forbes. Harding had appointed Forbes as director of the Veterans Bureau. The Veterans Bureau was in charge of taking care of the needs of former members of the U.S. military. Harding selected Forbes because he was a personal friend and had fought in World War I. Harding did not thoroughly investigate Forbes's past, however. He did not know that Forbes had deserted the Army and was arrested for another crime.[24]

Once in office, Forbes began to sell government medical supplies to private companies at incredibly low prices. Forbes also influenced contracts awarded for building new hospitals so that his friends would benefit. Harding learned of Forbes's behavior and demanded his resignation, privately calling him names.[25] However, President Harding did not publicly denounce Forbes or expose his criminal activities.

The Senate ordered a full-scale investigation of the Veterans Bureau in March 1923, two weeks after Forbes resigned. The scandal gained further attention when Charles F. Cramer, a lawyer at the Veterans Bureau, committed suicide. Cramer was an old friend of Forbes's and had worked closely with him while in office.

Jesse Smith, another friend of Harding's who worked for

the attorney general as a secretary, messenger, accountant, and campaign manager, was also found to have committed suicide in the summer of 1923.[26] Jesse Smith was on a first-name basis with the president, referring to him as "Warren." Smith used his direct access to the Bureau of Investigation and the Department of Justice to help businesses commit crimes like selling alcohol and avoiding prosecution.[27]

Smith set up a headquarters referred to as "the little green house on K Street" in Washington where he arranged deals giving people access to the Department of Justice. The "little green house" apparently earned up to $250,000 per deal. People would pay that much in order to receive favorable treatment in a court case or to avoid arrest for selling alcohol. Smith's suicide seemed to indicate that Harding and his administration were deeply tainted with corruption. This bad situation destroyed the president's morale. Harding and Daugherty tried their best to do their jobs as usual, to "return to normalcy," and to pretend that nothing was wrong. But the Smith, Daugherty, and Forbes scandals were only the beginning. The biggest scandal of the 1920s, Teapot Dome, was still to come.

chapter three

EVENTS LEADING UP TO TEAPOT DOME

BACKGROUND—In his book *The Origins of Teapot Dome*, historian J. Leonard Bates called the secretive sale of oil drilling permits at Teapot Dome "the greatest scandal of United States history."[1] Bates also said that the Teapot Dome scandal was filled with complications. For example, the name "Teapot Dome" refers to a limestone rock formation (not oil) in Wyoming near one of the oil reserves. The scandal itself also includes the oil reserves at Elk Hills and Buena Vista, California. The California sites were actually more productive oil deposits than the one in Wyoming, but reporters used the name "Teapot Dome" because it sounded more mysterious and scandalous than the names of the California locations.

The Teapot Dome scandal is also complicated by the vast number of people it involved. From President Harding down to mail clerks and custodians, people from all walks of life were involved in the scandal.

The Teapot Dome rock formation in Wyoming is near one of the oil reserves involved in the scandal.

Senators, environmental leaders, businesspeople, lawyers, petroleum industry leaders, reporters, bootleggers, and people in the Department of the Interior, the Department of Justice, and the Navy were all involved. The Teapot Dome scandal cast a large shadow over the entire decade of the 1920s. Historian and editor Bruce Bliven wrote that in order to have a scandal the size of Teapot Dome, three conditions must be in place:

> First, you must have a period of moral relaxation such as is common after a big war. Second, you must have a President in the White House who is complacent, ill-informed, and a poor judge of the integrity of his close friends. Third . . . the country must be unaware, before electing him, of these aspects of a nominee's character.[2]

Some historians labeled Harding the worst president of the twentieth century when evidence of illegal activities eventually became public. Journalist William Allen White said that Americans unfairly chose Harding to be president. After all, he was "weak, unprepared, [and] with no executive talent," and then he was put in the most powerful office in government.[3] People talked about scandals and corruption while Harding was in office because it seemed the country was running without much direction or enforcement of laws. Friends of President Harding used their influence with him to make a lot of money illegally.

According to historian Carl Sferrazza Anthony, President Harding created one of the ten worst White House scandals of all time.[4] The Teapot Dome scandal was a sensational case of public corruption and misjudgment during the 1920s. Some historians believe Teapot Dome was the scandal of the century. One historian wrote that Teapot Dome was one of the "four major scandals in American history" (the other three are the *Credit Mobilier* scandal in the Grant administration, Watergate of Nixon's presidency, and the Iran-Contra affair of President Reagan).[5] In comparison, though embarrassing, President Bill Clinton's impeachment and scandal involving Monica Lewinsky did not involve secret deals worth millions of dollars.

While Harding was president, Attorney General Harry M. Daugherty and his assistant Jesse Smith rented the little green house on K Street in Washington, D. C., where they kept liquor illegally, sometimes delivering it in official government vehicles with armed guards. Daugherty also accepted bribes from bootleggers, tried to get criminals out of jail, and pressured government officials who tried to enforce laws and prosecute cases. Daugherty, Smith, and their accomplices were known as the Ohio Gang. During the time the Ohio Gang operated in Washington, the money wasted in bribes could have been as high as $2 billion.[6]

Harding did not use good judgment in selecting people to serve with him in Washington. Harding's officials were called the Ohio Gang because they all seemed to be personal friends from the world of small-town Ohio politics. The editor of the *New Republic* wrote that Harding "brought with him to Washington one of the most astonishing collections of crooks, grafters, and black-mailers ever assembled."[7] Not all of Harding's Cabinet members were unqualified or from Ohio. For instance, Harding appointed the respected Charles Evans Hughes as secretary of state. He also appointed Herbert Hoover as secretary of commerce because of his knowledge of economics and business. Harding chose Andrew W. Mellon to be secretary of the treasury because Mellon was the most prominent and successful man in the financial world at that time.[8]

After Harding's death in 1923, many people began to hear rumors of mysterious deals, pardons, secret permits for the illegal sale of alcohol, gifts, "loans" to friends, and illegal profits from oil company stock. The director of the Veterans Bureau, Charles R. Forbes, had fled the country after embezzling (secretly stealing) $200 million in government funds. The Justice Department under Harry M. Daugherty accepted bribes and made money by selling confiscated alcohol.[9] A lawyer for the Veterans Bureau, Charles F. Cramer, shot himself. Jesse Smith, a corrupt assistant to Attorney General Daugherty, was found dead with a loaded gun beside him.[10]

The Teapot Dome scandal would destroy the reputations of many politicians in Washington for years to come. But what caused the scandal? In the early twentieth century after the Spanish-American War of 1898, ship engine technology changed from coal-burning steam turbine power to oil-burning turbines and diesel power. The Navy started converting its ships from coal-burning engines to more powerful oil-burning engines. Leaders of the Navy thought that their ships needed a more transportable fuel.[11] In 1909, President William Howard Taft set aside two sites of oil-rich deposits on federal land at Elk Hills and Buena Vista, California, for the U.S. Navy. President Woodrow Wilson created the third reserve at Teapot Dome, Wyoming, in 1916.

Three months after Warren Harding took office as president, he secretly transferred the oil reserves from the custody of the Navy to his close friend Albert B. Fall, secretary of the interior. In 1922, the year before Harding died, Albert B. Fall secretly leased the Teapot Dome, Wyoming, oil reserve to Harry F. Sinclair's Mammoth Oil Company and the Elk Hills, California, reserve to Edward Doheny's Pan-American Petroleum Company.[12]

Gifford Pinchot and Harry A. Slattery, two environmental leaders (called conservationists in the 1920s), were among the first people to question the interests of the administration of President Harding. Pinchot and Slattery

In 1909, President William Howard Taft set aside two sites of oil-rich deposits on federal land in California.

worked hard to find out how Harding would manage the forests, rivers, land, and natural resources of the country after he was elected in 1920.

Harry Slattery

Harry Slattery worked as a lawyer and environmental activist in Washington. He feared that President Harding's appointment of Albert B. Fall as secretary of the interior might lead to the government giving away too much access to private business. Instead of protecting the forests, waterways, and land, Fall might sell off rights to government-owned property.[13] Slattery knew about government agencies because he had worked in President Theodore Roosevelt's administration as a clerk. Slattery devoted himself to protecting the environment his whole life.

At first, Slattery thought Republicans like President Harding supported conservation. Slattery's friend Gifford Pinchot met with Harding to support him when he campaigned for the presidency.[14] Slattery and Pinchot thought that Harding would be a good president, and he would work to preserve the environment.

Gifford Pinchot

Gifford Pinchot got into trouble with President Taft in 1910 because of the Ballinger-Pinchot Controversy, an earlier, smaller version of the same mistakes that created the Teapot Dome scandal. Pinchot opposed selling Alaskan coal to private companies. As chief forester, Pinchot charged Secretary of the Interior Richard Ballinger with secretly negotiating business deals to sell the coal in Alaska.[15] President Taft supported Ballinger, and he demanded Pinchot's resignation.

Pinchot's resignation did not stop his environmental activism. Pinchot continued to exert enormous influence over environmental issues. His leadership helped to resolve the complicated Teapot Dome situation.

Albert B. Fall

If Pinchot and Slattery believed President Harding would protect the environment, everything changed when Harding appointed Albert B. Fall as secretary of the interior in 1921. So many people were involved in Teapot Dome that it is difficult to assign blame to one particular "villain." However, if one needed to name a villain, it might be Albert B. Fall. Fall spent time in prison in 1931 following his conviction for accepting $400,000 in bribes.[16]

Before he became secretary of the Interior, Albert B. Fall had served New Mexico as a senator. As a senator representing Ohio, Warren Harding sat next to Albert Fall in the Senate chambers. Fall later helped with Harding's presidential campaign. When Harding became president, he remembered Fall's tough reputation and rewarded his friendship by naming him to a position in the Cabinet.[17]

Born in Kentucky, Fall went out West to practice law in New Mexico before his election to the Senate. In New Mexico, Fall acquired ranch land, mine holdings, banks, and other business interests. With the income from his law practice and businesses, Fall began to build a considerable

Gifford Pinchot exerted enormous influence over environmental issues. His leadership helped to resolve the Teapot Dome scandal.

fortune. When the Senate formally investigated Teapot Dome in 1923, they found that Fall's New Mexico ranch had prospered at a time when the other ranches around his were failing. Apparently, Albert B. Fall had another source of income. Fall, like most westerners of the time, believed in the philosophy of "development." This meant ranching, mining, cutting down forests, building towns, and moving American Indians off their land. People heard rumors that Albert B. Fall had killed men in gunfights to protect his business interests.[18]

When Harding appointed Fall to his Cabinet, Slattery and Pinchot exchanged telegrams and letters about Harding's choice. Pinchot wrote, "it would have been possible to pick a worse man for Secretary of the Interior, but not altogether easy."[19] Another conservationist wrote, "Fall was condemned as absolutely unfit for such a post by every detail of his record in the Senate. He had been an exploiter . . . [who] always opposed the conservation movement."[20]

Albert B. Fall made a striking impression on people. His rags-to-riches success story impressed people. Fall

> wore a large black hat and a string tie; a cigar usually hung from the corner of his thin mouth; his eyes were narrow, blue, and cold . . . [and] he spoke with a drawl which could become disagreeably mean whenever he met opposition.[21]

Historian David H. Stratton wrote that Fall's "belief in the unrestrained disposition of the public lands was as typically Western as his black, broad-brimmed Stetson hat and his love of fine horses."[22]

Fall wanted to end what he saw as the mismanagement

Albert B. Fall made a striking impression on people, but not everyone was pleased with President Harding's choice of Fall as secretary of the Interior.

of resources. He wanted to bring the Navy's petroleum reserves under private management. Businesspeople soon realized Fall would be open to influence by business. If oil companies wanted to influence Fall's decisions with bribes and gifts, he would be willing to accept them.[23]

Edwin Denby

Harding's other Cabinet appointments also helped to pave the way for Teapot Dome. Harding's choice for secretary of the Navy was Edwin Denby. A conservative Republican, Denby had replaced the previous secretary, Josephus Daniels, who held very different views. It would be difficult to find two men more opposite than Denby and Daniels.

Daniels was a Democrat who fought for economic and social reforms considered radical in the 1920s. He supported union organization rights, child labor laws, and banning alcohol from the Navy. He later became a popular ambassador to Mexico.[24] President Harding appointed Edwin Denby to replace Daniels.

Denby came from a military background. During World War I, he served in the Marines, where he rose to the rank of major. As a career military man, Denby thought Daniels to be an ill-qualified newspaperman, "a landlubber who did not understand Navy traditions."[25]

As secretary of the Navy, Edwin Denby at first said that the Navy petroleum reserves must be kept intact. He did not want to change this policy, but he quickly changed his opinion under the influence of Albert B. Fall. Denby started to believe that it would be good to lease the three oil reserves, including Teapot Dome, to private companies.

Part of the reason for Denby's change of opinion was his vulnerable position. Denby was caught in the middle of a fight between two big government-run agencies, the Navy and the Department of the Interior. The Department of the Interior favored opening up western land for use. The Navy wanted the land held back. Even though some of his own advisors cautioned him against it, Denby decided to follow the recommendations of Secretary Fall instead of holding the oil reserves for the Navy.[26]

Denby felt he had many reasons for leasing the oil reserves. Buena Vista, Elk Hills, and Teapot Dome were being rapidly drained by oil wells on nearby land. A new leasing law permitted private companies to drill inside the California Navy oil reserves. If Fall leased the land, oil pumped by private companies would give the Navy the chance to earn money to build expensive above-ground storage tanks. The money made by selling the government-owned oil would fund these tanks. The oil storage tanks would give the Navy an emergency supply of fuel in case of war.

As the new boss of the Department of the Interior, Fall was ready to change the way business was done. No longer would the Navy tell the Department of the Interior how to handle government land. Fall eagerly sought the input of businesspeople and oil company executives in managing the reserves, and Denby put his "entire confidence" in Fall's ability to manage the reserves.[27] Fall proceeded rapidly with his new plan. He secretly negotiated deals without asking for several bids (as required by law). He challenged Pinchot and his ideas about protecting the environment. He proposed the opening of Alaska for development and attempted to transfer control of the national forests from the Department of Agriculture to his bureau. However, Fall failed in his effort to open Alaska. Pinchot and his supporters opposed it.[28]

Trying not to be discouraged by the "loss" of Alaska, Albert B. Fall transferred the three Navy oil reserves. On May 31, 1921, the oil fields were taken away from the Navy and given to the Department of the Interior. Fall achieved this transfer with the help of Secretary Denby and an executive order by President Harding. Then Fall called in his friends. He negotiated with Edward L. Doheny of the Pan-American Petroleum Company for drilling in California and for construction of storage tanks to be financed by oil profits. Shortly after this deal, Fall discussed with Harry F. Sinclair of Mammoth Oil Company the lease of Teapot Dome in 1922.[29]

Edward L. Doheny and Harry F. Sinclair

How did Doheny and Sinclair enter into the picture? Edward L. Doheny originally came to the West looking for gold and silver. He had grown up in a big Irish family in Wisconsin, and he left home at the age of sixteen hoping to make a lot of money. He became an expert in geology and drilled for oil in California. He drilled the first "gusher" to flow within the city of Los Angeles.[30] Doheny had about $100 million in oil holdings in the United States and

Mexico.[31] Albert B. Fall met Edward L. Doheny in 1886 when they were both looking for gold in New Mexico.

Fall knew Sinclair from his days as a rancher and miner in New Mexico.[32] Sinclair received the Teapot Dome lease for a minimum of twenty years. He could continue to extract oil and gas for as long as he liked if he could do so at a profit. Sinclair was supposed to pay the government 16 percent of his profits. If the reserves had been leased through competitive bidding, the government would have earned much more. Both Doheny and Sinclair expected to earn more than $100 million each, and their profits could run much higher since no one knew how much oil was in the ground at the three reserves.[33]

The *Wall Street Journal* carried a front-page report on April 14, 1921, announcing Fall's leasing of Teapot Dome to Sinclair's Mammoth Oil Company. The article stated, "[T]he arrangement . . . marks one of the greatest petroleum undertakings of the age and signalizes [sic] a notable departure on the part of the government in seeking partnership with private capital."[34] Suddenly, it looked as if the government no longer cared about protecting valuable natural resources from exploitation.

Environmental protectors like Pinchot, Slattery, and other government officials began to receive telegrams and letters from people upset by Albert B. Fall's decision. Senators John B. Kendrick of Wyoming, Robert La Follette of Wisconsin, and Thomas J. Walsh of Montana became aware of the sweeping changes taking place. Many Americans were concerned that Fall's new policy marked

Harry F. Sinclair, president of the Mammouth Oil Company received the Teapot Dome lease for twenty years. He was supposed to pay the government 16 percent of his profits.

a major change of attitude. They feared that important environmental and national defense issues were being ignored by a few greedy men. According to Bruce Bliven, "nothing could be more characteristic of the sickly moral atmosphere of the times than what happened when the three chief figures in the oil scandals [Fall, Sinclair, and Doheny] were brought into court."[35] But it would take many months of testimony and several court trials before Fall, Sinclair, and Doheny would face charges for their actions. Many people wanted to hide the evidence of Teapot Dome to protect the reputation of President Harding. The job of finding the evidence became very dangerous.

chapter four

SENATE HEARINGS FORCE OUT ALBERT B. FALL

SENATE HEARINGS— Conservationists Harry Slattery and Gifford Pinchot kept a watchful eye on the actions of Albert B. Fall. Three powerful senators— Robert M. La Follette of Wisconsin, John B. Kendrick of Wyoming, and Thomas J. Walsh of Montana—also soon joined Slattery and Pinchot in their efforts. With three senators in pursuit of Fall, he would eventually be forced to reveal secret information and resign in an attempt to avoid prosecution.

Since the day President Harding had appointed Albert B. Fall, Slattery wondered when Fall would try to turn his agency against the conservation movement. Slattery convinced Senator Robert M. "Fighting Bob" La Follette to help him gather information about Fall's secret dealings.

La Follette was a famous reform leader who successfully regulated industry. He helped to establish the first direct primary for elections in his home state.[1] Slattery suspected that Fall had already illegally sold government resources to

Albert B. Fall (right) was suspected of trying to turn his agency against the conservation movement.

private companies. Slattery wanted the Senate to force Fall to tell the truth. Senator La Follette began to search for facts. He was surprised to learn that no one in the Navy had criticized Fall's sale of the Teapot Dome oil reserves to Harry Sinclair's Mammoth Oil Company.[2]

La Follette began to get angry. President Harding's executive order giving Fall the right to sell the oil was made public only when the *Wall Street Journal* ran its article about it. The transfer had never been officially registered as required by the State Department. As Harry Slattery searched Washington for evidence of Fall's misdeeds, he talked with retired Navy energy expert Rear Admiral Robert S. Griffin. Griffin told Slattery, "if they get into this thing, they will find stranger things in heaven and earth than we have dreamed of."[3] Slattery told La Follette about his interview with Rear Admiral Griffin. The two supporters of conservation worked harder to find the "smoking gun" that would give proof of Fall's illegal activities.

News of Scandal Spreads

Senator John B. Kendrick began receiving telegrams and letters when news about the oil scandal appeared in the newspapers. Albert B. Fall still controlled the Department of the Interior, but rising suspicions were leading toward a debate in the Senate. Shortly after Fall leased Teapot Dome, he quickly leased the other reserves to Edward L. Doheny's Pan-American Petroleum Company in April 1922.[4]

Public Needs to Know the Facts

Congress endured many debates, resolutions, and official hearings about the secret transfer of the oil reserves. Wanting to stir up interest, Senator Kendrick introduced a Senate resolution on April 15, 1922. Kendrick said citizens of his home state needed to know the facts:

> The Secretary of the Interior and the Secretary of the Navy are negotiating with private parties for the operation of lands included in [naval petroleum reserves] . . . the interests of the State of Wyoming and . . . the people of the United States are so intimately involved in this matter . . . the public should be permitted to have some inkling of the terms upon which it is proposed to act. . . . Is it . . . to the interest of the Government to authorize the development of this field [and] to pay private operators for drilling the field?[5]

The Senate approved Kendrick's resolution without any comment. One week after The *Wall Street Journal* published news of the Teapot Dome lease, Senator La Follette submitted a strongly worded request to see published "a list of all oil leases made by the Department of the Interior within naval oil reserves . . . showing . . . the name of the lessee [and] the date of the lease."[6] La Follette wanted to hold Fall accountable, and he demanded records of all deals, contracts, accounting statements, and profit records.

Meanwhile, Albert B. Fall refused to explain or justify his two secret oil leases. La Follette decided to increase the pressure on Fall by calling for an official investigation. La Follette did not yet have enough facts to prove that Fall had committed any crime. Slattery and Pinchot gave Senator La Follette plenty of trustworthy information, but the senator needed hard facts, printed contracts, and letters from oil companies.

On April 28, 1922, La Follette gave one of the great speeches of his career. It was a savage and dramatic attack on Albert B. Fall. La Follette portrayed Secretary Fall as a "plunderer" and an aggressive "exploiter" of government property:

> all sorts of looting goes on in a Government as big as ours in spite of anything that can be done to prevent it. The most scandalous gouging of the public by private interests proba- bly occurs during a war period, and the plunderers operate through the War Department. But, sir, in normal peace times the sluiceway for a large part of the corruption to which this Government of ours is subjected is the Department of the Interior.[7]

La Follette argued that it was "almost unbelievable" that the secretary of the Navy would be willing to turn over these valuable resources to the Department of the Interior. Giving much praise to former Navy Secretary Josephus Daniels, the senator demon- strated how the country had moved from prudent conservation to willful neglect of the law. La Follette's speech

Robert La Follette recommended that an official hearing be held to look into the Teapot Dome situation.

leveled overwhelming accusations of the strange "mystery, evasions and denials" that Fall gave concerning his leases. The speech was so scathing that Republicans walked out of their side of the Senate chamber. One senator asked for a roll call so that the Republicans would be forced to return to hear the rest of La Follette's speech. Finally, the Senate (including thirty-nine Republicans) voted unanimously to adopt La Follette's recommendation for an official hearing.[8]

Investigations Begin

With the growing pressure of an official investigation ahead and the public outcry over his two oil leases, Albert B. Fall's days as secretary of the Interior were numbered. *The New York Times* reported that "overnight, Teapot Dome has become a matter of Congressional controversy which threatens to assume major proportions."[9] The investigation of Secretary Fall was assigned to the Senate Public Lands Committee (PLC) instead of the Naval Affairs Committee. (The Naval Affairs Committee would normally investigate any issue related to the Navy.) La Follette chose to give the investigation to the PLC because he wisely recognized that too many Republicans on the Naval Affairs Committee would try to stop an investigation.

The Senate hearing of the PLC began on October 22, 1923. Why did it take so long to begin when The *Wall Street Journal* had broken the story eighteen months earlier? Republicans on the PLC wanted to delay the start of the investigation with the hope that the public might lose inter-est in Teapot Dome. With elections coming up the following year, Republicans could lose many votes if their party were linked to corruption.

Meanwhile, Senator La Follette searched the PLC for senators who would be sympathetic to environmental issues. La Follette came upon Senator Thomas J. Walsh of Montana. Walsh eventually played a key role in untangling the mess of Teapot Dome, but at first, he showed little interest. As a westerner, Walsh understood Albert B. Fall's ranching, prospecting, and mining background. However, La Follette thought highly of Walsh's background in constitutional law. Walsh was an advocate of justice. Walsh's background and good reputation made him a perfect investigator into the confusion.

Historian Geoffrey Perrett wrote of Walsh, "there was no more devoted senator, nor a more intelligent one . . . He was a man who liked plain living, direct expression, and working sixteen hours a day."[10] Walsh was courageous and committed to fighting against corruption.

La Follette persuaded Walsh to take charge of the PLC and get Fall's secretive deals out in the open. Until La Follette talked with him, Walsh had not recognized the enormity of the Teapot Dome scandal.

Albert B. Fall Forced to Resign

Before the investigation began, La Follette and Kendrick made more charges against Albert B. Fall, forcing him to resign. La Follette argued in the Senate about an investigation into the high price of crude oil and gasoline. The senator wanted to find out if the oil companies had cooperated to artificially raise prices. La Follette read a letter from the Association of Oil Producers. They had passed resolutions of their own:

> Against the policy of any department of the Government
> . . . . entering into a contract . . . which would tend to con-
> tinue or perpetuate a monopolistic control of the oil industry
> of the United States or create a monopoly on the sale of fuel
> oil . . . The delivery of the naval reserves of the United States
> to the Standard Oil-Sinclair-Doheny interests constitutes a
> return to the era of land-grabbing and carpetbagging whose
> hydrohead of iniquity was crushed by the policy of President
> Roosevelt.[11]

These words made a big impression on Congress. Everyone remembered the sensational break up of the Standard Oil trust. During the nineteenth century, John D. Rockefeller had built the Standard Oil Company into a monopoly, a trust. A trust is a large corporation that controls many aspects of business such as banking, manufacturing, marketing, and labor. Standard Oil controlled 90 percent of the petroleum market by 1880. President Theodore Roosevelt worked to enforce antitrust laws, and he broke up Standard Oil in 1907, saying, "There is a widespread con-viction in the minds of the American people that the great corporations known as trusts are . . . hurtful to the general welfare."[12]

Suspicions against big business helped to create support for La Follette's investigation into Albert Fall and Teapot Dome. The threat of Senate hearings drove Fall out of office. On January 2, 1923, eight months after the Senate's approval of La Follette's request for an investigation, Fall

Theodore Roosevelt, the twenty-sixth president of the United States (standing behind striped flag), worked to keep large corporations from hurting the general welfare of the country.

resigned as secretary of the Interior. He claimed that he was resigning because he wanted to devote more time to his businesses in New Mexico. More likely, however, Fall wanted to influence politics in his home state, with the threat of a Senate investigation looming.[13]

According to one journalist, Fall did not resign willingly but was forced out by President Harding. Harding was attempting to clean up his reputation and break away from his corrupt past by asking Fall to leave.[14] Harding wanted to restore his political reputation before the 1924 primaries and election. If Harding got rid of Fall, the Democrats would have less ammunition to use in their campaign.

President Harding's Problems Show

Between January and August 1923, Harding's troubles increased as more and more rumors of corruption surfaced. Harding was under a great deal of stress. His worries about the activities of the Ohio Gang kept him up at night. When he died on August 2, 1923, Vice President Calvin Coolidge was named president. Two major players in Teapot Dome, Warren Harding and Albert Fall, were gone from Washington, but the scandal was still slowly unfolding.

When the PLC hearing began on October 23, 1923, Albert B. Fall was the first witness to testify. The main targets of the investigation would be Fall, Harry F. Sinclair, and Edwin Denby, the secretary of the Navy. Reporters crammed into the Senate Office Building expecting fireworks and sensational arguments. Fall answered Walsh's questions with "more than his usual touch of quiet arrogance."[15] He tried to argue that he had done nothing wrong. He said he was protecting the best interests of the American people by leasing the oil fields. He insisted that President Harding had complete authority to authorize the transfer of the oil deposits. However, Walsh forced Fall to admit he sought no advice from lawyers and had not asked for competitive bids before leasing the oil to private companies.

> **Walsh:** I wanted to ask you if you called for competitive bids when you sought to lease Teapot Dome?
>
> **Fall:** No, sir; but I did when I sought, at the request of the Navy, to make further leases upon these oil reserves in California . . . I give you my reasons there in that report.

Walsh: Your reasons why you did not call for bids on the Teapot Dome?

Fall: No, sir; my reasons as to the difference in the two situations. In the California naval reserve there were developments. There were refineries, competitive refineries, immediately around. . . . In the Teapot Dome there is no such situation. There was practically an absolute monopoly in Midwest Co. in that field at that time.

Walsh: Then your reason for not calling for bids was what?

Fall: Well, I will get to that, if you want that. Are you asking me now for my reason for not calling for bids on the Teapot Dome?

Walsh: Yes.

Fall: Business, purely. Because I knew I could make a better price without calling for bids.[16]

At another point in the testimony, Walsh wanted to show how Fall had violated the law. The oil leases were illegal in at least two ways: First, Fall had signed them secretly, without competitive bidding. Second, he had accepted bribes for signing the leases. Walsh read aloud the section of the law requiring that any service or supply provided to the government had to be advertised. The law made an exception for "personal services." Those did not need to be advertised. Fall attempted to fight back against Walsh's questions.

Fall: Are you calling my attention to that statute?

Walsh: Yes.

Fall: You do not mean to say that that statute would prohibit the Secretary of the Navy from making a private contract with reference to handling naval property, do you?

Walsh: Why, would you not think so?

Fall: No; I do not.

Walsh: Why not?

Fall: Well, because I do not. I do not think it is applicable at all.

Walsh: Why is it not applicable?

Fall: Well, why is it applicable?

Fall: Oh, yes; it is personal service if service at all. Let us get now what you mean. Is the Navy operating naval reserves now itself; and if so, is it not by the personal service of those persons who are drilling wells and producing oil? Is not that true?

Walsh: Why, Senator, personal service, you understand perfectly well, is rendered by a clerk or an employee down at one of the departments, for instance.[17]

Fall did his best to try to fight off Walsh's questions. He resented having to testify, and he was stubborn in his answers. Many times, he would restate the question asked by Walsh. Fall thought he was being asked to testify for political rather than legal reasons, and he resented the humiliation.

Walsh knew that he had to find evidence in the form of money, bribes, contracts, and other factual information that would expose Secretary Fall's corruption. After reviewing the size of the Teapot Dome reserve, Walsh said, "[Y]ou understood that Mr. Sinclair paid $1,000,000 to get this?" Fall admitted this was true, but hesitated to point out "the contract was not drawn by Mr. Sinclair" but by the Department of the Interior. Fall claimed the lease "would require of anyone before a lease was made a surrender of all claim of interest of any kind . . . particularly, of course, as to those which I regarded as a menace."[18]

Because of the technical nature of the debate about laws over land use, people quickly began to lose interest in the Senate hearings. After the first day of testimony, *The New York Times* reported, "[T]he hearings will be continued tomorrow, but all interest in its outcome has evaporated with the reports of experts."[19] Fall's strategy had been to flood the PLC with truckloads of documents that would make it impossible to figure out what exactly was illegal.

Fall testified for two days and sometimes debated with and seemed aggravated by Senator Walsh. Fall kept returning to the idea of himself as a patriotic businessman who was helping the military readiness of the country. Walsh kept pursuing Fall with dogged determination. He was trying to get Fall to confess to wrongdoing, but the hearing produced no real evidence of Fall's corruption. Senator Walsh seemed to be fighting against Fall, Denby, and Sinclair all by himself. Walsh also received anonymous death threats against his daughter while the investigation dragged on. An unidentified man grabbed Walsh's daughter while she was out walking and threatened her life if the investigation continued. Some suspected that the Bureau of Investigation (later called the FBI) under Harry Daugherty was behind this intimidation of Walsh and his family.[20]

Walsh eventually got tired of the Senate hearings, and he seemed ready to abandon his search. Then Harry Slattery talked with Senator Walsh again, and he reminded Walsh that the PLC hearings were highly political. Slattery gave

Walsh a list of possible witnesses—people who would know a lot about Teapot Dome.[21] Suddenly Walsh realized the huge political dimension of Teapot Dome.

The investigation was not only about oil and Secretary Fall but also about the Republican party itself, which could be seriously damaged. If any of the oil companies had donated to Republican campaigns, the Democrats could charge that the Republicans were bought by corrupt oil businessmen. Democratic National Committee Chairman Cordell Hull said in *The New York Times*, "in all its history, the Democratic Party has never been disgraced by such a scandal as the secret lease of Teapot Dome."[22] The use of the word *scandal* by Hull seems to indicate that the word was becoming commonly used. When people thought of Fall, Harding, Teapot Dome, and the Republicans, they thought of scandal.

Pursuit of Truth Continues

Public interest gathered new momentum and Walsh experienced renewed energy in his pursuit of the truth. Walsh's sense of getting closer to a big break occurred when a newspaper from New Mexico reported that Albert B. Fall had made substantial improvements on his ranch in New Mexico. Where had Fall gotten the money? Before the oil leases, Fall's ranch had been typical of the area, but now it had luxurious additions and new livestock. Walsh called in Fall's ranch manager, who testified that Harry Sinclair visited Fall's ranch and gave him cows. Sinclair denied giving any bribe in order to win an oil contract from Fall.

Under oath, Edwin Denby and Albert B. Fall denied any anticompetitive agreement concerning the oil leases.

Earlier, Fall had sent a statement to PLC chairman Reed Smoot about his finances. Fall claimed he had borrowed $100,000 from Edward R. McLean, publisher of *The Washington Post*, in order to enlarge his ranch. Walsh suspected that his money came not from the newspaper world but was laundered" money from Sinclair or Doheny. If the oil companies gave the money to McLean, he could give it to Fall without any hint of the real source.

During the hearings, Fall experienced health problems, and he left Washington for Florida where he stayed with Edward McLean. The Democrats sensed that political advantage could be gained by emphasizing Fall's flight to Florida. People began to demand that Fall needed to tell the truth about the money he used to improve his ranch. The Republicans, however, began to fear that the truth might be more damaging than Fall's refusal to testify.

Edward Doheny's Stunning Confession

In January 1924, Edward Doheny calmly confessed that he, not Edward McLean, had "loaned" Fall the money.[23] The truth was finally out in the open. Doheny told the PLC that his son had carried the money to Fall's office "in a little black bag." Walsh had finally been able to catch Fall in a lie. (Fall claimed the money came from McLean.) The Democrats celebrated the fact that Fall had been caught lying. The Republicans feared that Fall's immoral behavior would drag down President Coolidge, who now tried to distance himself from the ill will associated with Teapot Dome.

Doheny's confession about the bribe was not, however, the most dramatic testimony. The most famous break in the case came when Archie Roosevelt took the stand on January 21, 1924. Archie was the son of the former Rough Rider, President Theodore Roosevelt, so people were very interested in his point of view. A former employee of Sinclair's Mammoth Oil Company, Archie resigned from his job the day before he testified. Archie told the PLC that the day after Senator Walsh questioned Edward McLean, Sinclair asked him to buy a ticket on a steamship leaving for Paris in three days.[24] Sinclair's desire to avoid punishment by quickly leaving for France implied guilt.

After Archie Roosevelt's testimony, many newspapers sent reporters to Washington. The public had a renewed fascination with Teapot Dome. *The New York Times* reported that Archie Roosevelt "turned what had been a somewhat tiresome investigation into a national sensation."[25] With the confessions of Edward Doheny and Archie Roosevelt, Walsh succeeded in turning the hearing into a full-speed force that would crush anyone unlucky enough to be in its path. Instead of just rumors, now Walsh had found real confessions and real evidence of wrongdoing. People connected with Teapot Dome had tried to hide the truth and avoid prosecution. Nobody was safe now. Any possible connection with Fall and his secret dealings would be enough to permanently ruin the career of any politician.

Many Republicans worried about the public's

Archie Roosevelt took the stand during the Teapot Dome trial. He was the son of the former Rough Rider, President Theodore Roosevelt (shown here on horseback).

impression of Teapot Dome. President Coolidge and Vice President Hoover were concerned that elections were just a few short months away. The Senate hearing continued to produce more confessions of bribes, lies, and double-deals. Eventually, the testimony revealed that Doheny and Sinclair gave Fall nearly $400,000 in loans and bribes. Fall would spend a year in jail (but not until 1931, after a second round of hearings). Republicans tried to limit the damage by calling Teapot Dome "the Fall case." Democrats, on the other hand, exaggerated the impact. The great task facing President Coolidge was to lead the nation out of its obsession with Teapot Dome. Coolidge needed to convince citizens that there were still honest people in government and that the laws would be enforced:

> It is not for the President to determine criminal guilt or render judgment in civil causes; that is the function of the courts. It is not for him to prejudge. I shall do neither. . . . If there has been any crime, it must be prosecuted. If there has been any property of the United States illegally transferred or leased, it must be recovered. . . . If there is any guilt it will be punished; if there is any civil liability it will be enforced; if there is any fraud it will be revealed; and if there are any contracts which are illegal they will be cancelled.[26]

chapter five

TEAPOT DOME SMEARS ITS NEXT VICTIMS

MORE VICTIMS—Many Americans wondered when the mystery of Teapot Dome would end. The testimony of witnesses at the Senate PLC hearings continued. Senator Walsh had uncovered important clues in getting Secretary of the Interior Albert B. Fall to resign. However, many questions still remained unanswered. For instance, where did the corruption begin? Had President Harding ordered all the oil leases and deals? What happened to all the money paid out by the oil companies? Which politicians accepted bribes in return for favorable treatment by the Justice Department?

The Search Continues

As the investigation gained momentum, the PLC hearings became more intense. Anyone, guilty or innocent, Republican or Democrat, might be identified as a target. Even a casual association with Teapot Dome could end the career of a prominent politician. Senator Walsh and the PLC seemed to gain power from the serious accusations being made against former associates of Harding's.

One question lingered in the background, but no one had asked it yet. "Did Walsh have enough power to topple the President himself?" First, Walsh needed to demonstrate that President Coolidge had had previous knowledge of illegal activities.

Edwin Denby in the Spotlight

Suspicions began to swirl around Edwin Denby, the secretary of the Navy appointed by Warren Harding. On January 28, 1924, the Senate debated a resolution demanding that President Coolidge remove Denby from his job.

House Democrat Finis J. Garrett said that the past few days of testimony "uncovered probably the most shameful chapter ever written into the history of this Republic." Garrett declared that recent revelations had "shaken the faith of the country in the Government."[1] Senator J. Thomas Heflin of Alabama also harshly criticized the behavior of Harding's Cabinet:

> I do not charge these crooked and corrupt doings to the rank and file of the Republican Party, but I am holding responsible Republican officials who have been unfaithful and who have proven themselves unworthy of the trust reposed in them. . . . There seems to be corruption in practically every department of the Government. . . . This Teapot Dome scandal is not an isolated case. . . . The whole atmosphere is permeated with suggestions of scandal, and I want to go to the bottom of all of them.[2]

President Calvin Coolidge worried that the public's impression of Teapot Dome might affect the upcoming election.

After the resignation of Albert B. Fall, the secretary of the Navy became the most sought-after scapegoat. In this case, a scapegoat would be a public official who got stuck with all the blame even though many people were involved in the scandal. With the way the testimony was unfolding, people knew Denby would not be in office much longer. Even the Republican members of Congress did not want to defend Edwin Denby against the mostly Democratic attack directed by Senator Walsh.

Denby told the PLC that he would not resign because he thought the oil leases were legal.[3] Even when Senator Walsh criticized him for giving the oil reserves to the secretary of the Interior, Denby fought hard against any charges of wrongdoing. Walsh challenged Denby in the Senate hearings. Walsh demanded that unless Denby resigned his position, he would "ask action by this body appropriate to the occasion."[4] President Coolidge was directed by the Senate to begin legal proceedings to cancel the oil leases to Sinclair and Doheny.

Meanwhile, Senator George H. Moses declared that the investigation would continue. Moses said that the Senate would witness "partisan snipers making a rifle pit of the grave of Warren Harding," meaning that people associated with Teapot Dome would go down in disgrace along with Harding.[5] Nobody would respect anyone connected with Teapot Dome. One newspaper reporter said, "All over Washington there is a feeling that the worst is yet to come." Another wrote that Coolidge's entire Cabinet should resign to allow the president to clear the air and make a fresh start without the taint of past crimes.[6]

President Coolidge reacted slowly to the demands of the Senate. He refused to be bullied by the anger sweeping the country. He calmly stated he would not ask for the resignations of his entire Cabinet but he would pursue the truth.

However, Coolidge would "not hesitate to call for the resignation of any official whose conduct . . . warrants such action." Coolidge would "act upon the evidence and the law" as he found it and "deal thoroughly . . . with every kind of wrong doing."[7] The president needed to appear in control and not seem bossed around by Walsh, the Senate, or the PLC. Coolidge refused to fire Denby quickly and without cause. This brought praise from the Republicans and complaints from the Democrats.

Even though Coolidge refused to fire Denby, the secretary of the Navy decided to resign on his own on February 18. Denby never admitted to doing anything wrong. He insisted all along that the oil leases were legal. He claimed that he quit only to save Coolidge from the lengthy, embarrassing arguments in the Senate. With Denby's resignation, the full force of the PLC investigation would seek out its next victim, Attorney General Harry Daugherty.

In newspapers, on the radio, in hotels, coffee shops, offices, churches, and at family dinner tables, the Teapot Dome scandal was being discussed. Journalist Bruce Bliven wrote, nobody "cared about Teapot Dome when it was a question of conservation; only when it became a scandal of personalities and corruption" did people suddenly perk up with fascination.[8]

Conservation had failed to interest people because most citizens at that time thought America had an endless supply of natural resources. But political scandal was another matter. Personalities, gossip, rumors, scandals, and dramatic Senate hearings were entertainment.

Politicians Fear Connection to Teapot Dome

What did Attorney General Harry Daugherty have to hide? Everybody knew he was a friend of Harry Sinclair and Edward Doheny, the owners of the oil companies. The Justice Department had provided no evidence or cooperation during the hearings of the PLC when it was asked about Sinclair and Doheny, so people knew Daugherty was hiding illegal activity. One political cartoon of the time showed a fat Daugherty with his back pressed hard against a closet door. Behind the door, a ghastly crew of skeletons pushed hard to knock down the door. On the skeletons' heads were written the names of various scandals such as "war," "fraud," and "Teapot Dome."[9]

Daugherty did not prosecute criminals who illegally sold alcohol, and his offices prevented bribery cases from coming to trial. Several Republican leaders went to President Coolidge and told him "Daugherty should retire for the good of the party."[10]

Denby and Fall had resigned the offices given to them by Harding, and Daugherty's head was next on the chopping block. With the Teapot Dome scandal reaching full speed like a train gaining momentum down a mountain, it was only a matter of time before Daugherty was fired. The only questions left were what evidence was needed to damage Daugherty's credibility, and who else would be implicated in his prosecution. The investigation seemed to have no limits.

With all the news and testimony, President Coolidge began to look at the damage to his political career. He defended Denby and stood by his Cabinet, and he also bravely defended the newly assaulted Daugherty. Originally, Daugherty offered to resign immediately after Coolidge became president. Coolidge, however, refused to accept the resignation. Losing any Cabinet member would give the impression that Harding's friends had abandoned him. Coolidge told Herbert Hoover he planned to make no Cabinet changes after Harding's death.

Daugherty stood firm against the Teapot Dome investigation. Meanwhile, many Democratic senators verbally attacked the attorney general, the scandal, and the President who sheltered him. On March 1, the Senate passed a resolution demanding Daugherty's resignation for his failure to prosecute Fall, Sinclair, and Doheny.

A special investigation committee heard testimony from the wife of the late Jesse Smith, who had died suspiciously. Smith's wife told of secret oil deals, special treatment by the Justice Department, speculation in oil stocks, and other illegal activities led by Daugherty.[11]

As the evidence piled up, President Coolidge felt he finally needed to take action and fire the attorney general.

Daugherty's terrible reputation prevented Coolidge from focusing on his job of running the country. Daugherty received the message from Coolidge, and he resigned. Daugherty later said, "I'm just a private citizen out of a job. . . . I hope lies told by irresponsible so-called witnesses as to immoral conduct, disgraceful doings and improper associations on my part will not be believed."[12]

The Teapot Dome scandal had forced the president to get rid of Daugherty. Next, President Coolidge struggled to clean himself of the stain of oil, especially during the election year of 1924. Three Harding appointees had been removed from office. This reduced the stress on the Republicans and President Coolidge. However, fear of more investigations was never far away. *The New York Times* stated that "having disposed of Attorney General Daugherty as well as Secretary Denby," the Senate considered investigating Secretary of Commerce Andrew W. Mellon. Mellon was suspected of holding office in violation of a law that "forbids the Treasury head to be engaged in trade or commerce."[13]

Another bizarre twist in the Teapot Dome investigation emerged when C. Bascom Slemp, the private secretary of President Coolidge, faced the questioning of Senator Walsh. Slemp had been with Albert B. Fall when Fall visited newspaper publisher Edward McLean. Slemp claimed he knew nothing of the $100,000 "loan." When Walsh asked Slemp if he had spoken with Coolidge in the company of Fall or McLean, Slemp refused to answer directly. Walsh then produced a pile of telegrams that Coolidge had received from

Slemp. Some of these telegrams were written in a secret code used by the Justice Department. Deciphering the wacky spelling provided an exciting pastime for reporters who tried to figure out sentences like "Jaguar baptisical stowage beadle 1235 huff pulsator commensal fifful."[14] Jaguar turned out to be the code word for Senator Walsh. The sentence says that Walsh is out of town and Slemp wants to know with whom to confer. Coolidge did send one telegraph directly to McLean, but it did not reveal any illegal evidence or convict the president of any crime. The mystery of the reasoning behind using a secret code remains unknown to this day.

Coolidge explained that his telegrams to McLean were legitimate and not related to Teapot Dome. However, Slemp's telegrams provided yet more information for the reporters. A newspaper in Philadelphia said that the secret telegrams showed "a strikingly clear impression of the unwholesome atmosphere which has pervaded the Capital." *The New York Times* described it as "humiliating to think that we have come to the point where every idle tale and gratuitous suspicion about the President . . . must be given resounding publicity."[15] But not everyone agreed that Coolidge should be publicly attacked and linked to Harding's mistakes. Henry Cabot Lodge, a Republican senator from Massachusetts, defended Coolidge and said attacks against the president showed disrespect for the nation.

As the investigation continued, Senator Walsh looked for more firm evidence of conspiracy. He tried to show that

Senator Henry Cabot Lodge of Massachusetts (shown here) said the attacks against President Coolidge showed disrespect for the nation.

Republicans had planned to use oil money as far back as the 1920 convention. One of the Republican candidates for president, General Leonard Wood, had told conservationist Gifford Pinchot he could get the nomination if he agreed to sell government oil.[16]

The Investigation Continues

Many witnesses came to Washington to testify. Some of the strangest information came from a reformed train robber named Al Jennings. He told the PLC that in 1920 when the Republican party decided to nominate Harding for president, Harding had paid the Republicans $1 million. Harding's money came from the oil companies in a deal engineered by an "ex-Senator."[17] *The New York Times* reported that seventy-five thousand shares of Sinclair oil stock helped the Republican party pay off 1920 campaign debts. No firm evidence of these sensational charges ever surfaced, however.

By May 1924, as the Teapot Dome investigation dragged on, people grew tired of reading about it. Newspapers were not reporting as much about it. The end of the investigation was near. Federal courts in Wyoming and California issued orders that stopped further oil drilling at Elk Hills and Teapot Dome. Special prosecutors filed lawsuits against Sinclair's Mammoth Oil Company and Doheny's Pan-American Petroleum Company.

The Republican party had endured one of the worst periods in its history. How would President Coolidge survive this scandal? Coolidge's biographers show him to be upset with the political legacy he inherited, but he was amazingly calm. He kept an appearance of honesty during all the months of testimony. He rid himself of Fall, Denby, and Daugherty, the three biggest liabilities and links to the corruption. Coolidge replaced the fallen, corrupt administrators with competent new officials. He appointed Curtis D. Wilber as secretary of the Navy and Harlan Fiske Stone as attorney general. People thought Wilber and Stone were more qualified and better appointees than Denby and Daugherty.[18]

Coolidge also helped distance himself from the scandal and control its impact by starting the Federal Oil Conservation Board, which regulates oil drilling, processing, sales, and exports.

Coolidge appointed special counsels, lawyers Owen J. Roberts and Atlee Pomerene, to clean up the mess created by Teapot Dome. He gave Roberts and Pomerene unlimited authority to handle prosecution of those connected to the illegal oil leases.

During the hundreds of hours of testimony, no absolutely clear evidence ever emerged to link Coolidge with Teapot Dome. Coolidge held on through the furious assault directed at him by Senator Walsh. The final report of the investigation would allow some of the scandal to fade away. Coolidge could focus on restoring his party's reputation and winning reelection. It appeared the oil stain would not leave a permanent mark on Coolidge's reputation.

chapter six

TEAPOT DOME AND THE ELECTION OF 1924

ELECTION NEARS— Before the presidential election in 1924, the three major political parties of the 1920s—the Republicans, the Democrats, and the Progressives—had different plans for dealing with the lessons of Teapot Dome. The Republicans, who had been linked to Teapot Dome from the beginning, tried to minimize the significance of the scandal. The other two parties saw a chance to win the election by highlighting the supposed Republican corruption.

The nomination of President Coolidge by Republicans was not a dramatic event. The Republican party dominated the 1920s despite Teapot Dome. The Republicans stressed prosperity, a healthy economy, stability, and harmony in the campaign of 1924. Past scandals seemed un-important when a tax cut and economic prosperity were mentioned. Coolidge had inherited the presidency when Warren G. Harding died. Coolidge's reputation as a tough, independent, and respectable New England politician distanced him from Harding's scandals.[1] Coolidge appeared to be able to guarantee prosperity and virtue. One businessman wrote, "[Coolidge] is just what the country needs, a quiet, simple, unobtrusive man, with no isms and no desire for any reform. The business world needs to be let alone to recover from the war strain and governmental interference in business."[2]

With the Republican Teapot Dome scandal behind them, the Democrats should have had an easy time capturing the White House. However, they had problems in their party. The Democrats had divided up into special interest groups after Woodrow Wilson left office in 1920. One faction of the Democratic party focused on the rural South and the West. The other faction was made up of Democrats in the fast-growing cities of the North and Midwest like Philadelphia and Chicago.

The Democratic Party Splits

A new industrial revolution swept across the North and Midwest as the cities increased in size. Factories, railroad networks, immigration, and union movements created a new kind of Democrat in the North.[3] On the other hand, Democrats in the South and the West who had previously supported Wilson stood for prohibition of alcohol, fundamentalist religion, tolerance of the Ku Klux Klan (KKK), and support for agriculture and traditional values.

The KKK believed in the supremacy of the Caucasian (white) race and segregation of African Americans. The northern Democrats were influenced by labor unions and the recent immigration of European Catholics and Jews. They opposed Prohibition and religious extremism, and they tried to turn the party in a new direction.[4] The new Democrats promoted labor unions, equal opportunity, and the rights of workers.

The split within the Democratic party prevented the organization from capitalizing on Teapot Dome. When the party met for its national convention in New York, the meeting degenerated into a "snarling, cursing, tenuous, suicidal, homicidal roughhouse." An urban resolution to condemn the KKK led to a violent reaction from the rural delegates, and the measure was defeated by a single vote.[5]

The Democratic National Convention dragged on in New York. The Democrats could not agree on the best person to nominate to try to defeat Coolidge. The urban delegates from the Midwest and Northeast liked Alfred E. Smith, the governor of New York. The rural delegates from the South and West liked William Gibbs McAdoo of California. But McAdoo had been caught up in the Teapot Dome scandal. During the Senate hearings, Edward Doheny testified that he had paid McAdoo's law firm to help negotiate oil deals in Mexico. McAdoo tried furiously to deny any involvement in Teapot Dome, but nobody believed him.

Neither the urban nor the rural Democratic candidate could win a majority within the party, so the Democrats kept looking. On the 103rd ballot, they finally settled on John W. Davis, a former West Virginia congressman. Davis was a compromise candidate just as Harding had been in 1920.

Divisions within the Democratic party, however, kept Davis from using Teapot Dome to his advantage.

The Progressive Party

The Progressives believed in government ownership of railroads, legalizing unions strikes, and freedom of farmers to organize collectively and set prices. These beliefs were not radically different from the Democratic party of the time. The Progressive party brought together farm workers, union members, socialists, and other reform-minded citizens. Progressives generally viewed Teapot Dome as evidence of the immoral excesses of unregulated business and corrupt government.

The Progressives nominated Robert M. La Follette of Wisconsin, who had been the first senator to bring the Teapot Dome scandal to national attention. La Follette liked to fire up crowds with long speeches denouncing the corruption in government.

The Progressives and Democrats called for new measures to clean up government, create a better society, regulate business, and prevent another

The Progressives nominated Robert La Follette of Wisconsin as their candidate for the presidential election of 1924.

Teapot Dome scandal from happening. However, many Americans liked Coolidge better because he made no big promises like those made by reformers. Coolidge's conservative, quiet, small-town character reminded people of the reasons they had elected Harding. Even with the uncertain outcome of lawsuits and court decisions about Teapot Dome, people thought that Coolidge had nothing to do with the oil scandal. Coolidge managed to stay miraculously free and clear of the accusations.

Of the three men running for president (Coolidge, Davis, and La Follette), Coolidge seemed to best fit the needs of the voting public in 1924. He used his unimpressive, soft-spoken style in radio addresses in which he promoted "nonpartisan" views. A photograph appeared in many newspapers showing Coolidge baling hay with a pitchfork. This simple physical labor symbolized tradition and the American values of home, morality, and decency.[6] Coolidge seemed innocent of scandal while the Democrat Davis dealt with the touchy KKK issue. As a Progressive, La Follette strongly denounced Teapot Dome. In the election, La Follette managed to gain a following among urban working people and immigrant groups, and he won 17 percent of the popular vote. Coolidge easily won reelection with 54 percent, while Davis took just under 29 percent of the vote.[7]

Coolidge could now focus his energy on running the country. For a while, the scandal disappeared from newspaper headlines because the Senate hearings were over. The unfinished business of the questionable oil leases eventually ended up in court. The oil scandal led to many civil and

Of the three men running for president in 1924 Coolidge (shown here in the center panning for gold) seemed to best fit the needs of the voting public.

criminal legal cases. Several of those cases reached the United States Supreme Court. The civil cases concerned the validity of the oil leases to Doheny and Sinclair. The criminal cases examined which laws were broken by Fall, Sinclair, Doheny, and others in bribes, unfair bargains, and secret deals in getting the oil leases.

The First Teapot Dome Oil Court Case

The first oil case to reach a courtroom trial was the civil suit to cancel the Elk Hills lease to Doheny's Pan-American Petroleum Company. The trial began on October 21, 1924, in United States District Court in Los Angeles. The public seemed to favor Fall and Doheny. Some people believed that Fall and Doheny had been victimized by the government. However, Prosecutor Owen Roberts argued that Albert B. Fall had given his friend Doheny preferential treatment, made secret deals, and received bribes as incentive.

The defense tried to argue that Doheny had full authority to write contracts to sell government oil. They tried to make Doheny look like a patriotic citizen. The star witness for the defense was an admiral from the Navy. He testified about his fear that the Navy would lose its oil to nearby wells and that we could lose a war in the Pacific without proper oil reserves to power ships. Admiral Robison claimed he begged Doheny to build oil storage tanks at Pearl Harbor that would provide the Navy with energy in the event of an attack from the East.

In the end, Judge Paul J. McCormick's 105-page decision said that the lease to Elk Hills and the contract for storage tanks at Pearl Harbor were invalid because they were accomplished through fraud, conspiracy, and bribes.[8] Doheny's company was ordered to pay the government for all the oil it had taken out of Elk Hills. McCormick said the purpose of the secrecy in the lease was to prevent Congress and the American people from knowing the truth, not to protect national security.

More Teapot Dome Oil Court Cases

The civil suit to cancel Harry Sinclair's lease to Teapot Dome began in Cheyenne, Wyoming, on March 9, 1925. During the weeks leading up to the trial, many people associated with Teapot Dome and curious spectators began to fill up the quiet frontier town. Normally only a rodeo drew such a large crowd in Cheyenne. Harry Sinclair arrived with several famous, highly paid attorneys from Washington and New York.[9]

Special prosecutors Roberts and Atlee Pomerene subpoenaed Albert B. Fall as a witness in this second civil trial. A subpoena is an order legally requiring a person to appear in court with the threat of a penalty (such as a fee or jail time) for failure to comply. Fall had gotten older and "His hair and drooping mustache were now white; he had lost weight and his clothes seemed to hang on him."[10] Fall's ill health caused the judge to view him more sympathetically. Sinclair's attorneys tried to prove that the only payment Sinclair made to Fall was $25,000 in bonds for his trip to Russia in 1923, well after the Teapot Dome lease had been signed. One of the defense attorneys, an especially good speaker, portrayed Fall as a hunted victim desperate to escape the aggressive tactics of the Senate.

In their closing argument for the government, Pomerene and Roberts ridiculed the idea that national security depended on the transfer of the oil leases. However, Sinclair's high-powered legal team had captured the attention of the judge, T. Barry Kennedy. The government lost the first Teapot Dome court case. Despite losing, Roberts and Pomerene established the fraudulent character of Doheny's Continental Trading Company, which had served as a false business front to hide illegal activity.

In this trial, Judge T. Barry Kennedy ruled against the

government and upheld the legality of President Harding's executive order transferring Teapot Dome to Fall. Judge Kennedy stated that the Departments of the Interior and Navy had full authority to lease Teapot Dome, and he denied the lease had been made through bribery. Kennedy regarded the contracts as "fairly and honestly carried out," and thought they "will actually conserve oil which would otherwise have been lost."[11] He wrote:

> The great general public is reached only with the sensational features surrounding the transactions involved and, being largely in the dark as to all the other multitude of circumstances with which the case is surrounded and knowing perhaps less of the great legal principles which the experience of the ages has taught mankind must control in dealing with the rights of persons and property.[12]

Decision Overturned

The statement's insulting tone angered many people who thought that the millionaires had beaten the system again. The government appealed the case. In September 1926, the United States Circuit Court of Appeals in St. Louis reversed Judge Kennedy's decision. The circuit court declared the Teapot Dome lease invalid because it was negotiated with fraud. Fall received a bribe from Sinclair, and this was a serious accusation against a public official ignored by Judge Kennedy in the Cheyenne trial.[13]

Meanwhile, Doheny appealed the Elk Hills decision against him in Los Angeles in October 1925. Three judges upheld Judge McCormick's decision. But they reversed his decision that Doheny's company was entitled to money it had already paid to build oil storage tanks at Pearl Harbor. Doheny appealed this second decision to the United States Supreme Court. The government won both on Doheny's appeal from the Elk Hills decision in California and on its own appeal from the Teapot Dome decision.

On February 28, 1927, the Supreme Court unanimously cancelled Doheny's lease to Teapot Dome and refused to order payment by the government for any money spent by Doheny. On October 10, 1927, the Supreme Court unanimously restored Teapot Dome to complete ownership by the federal government. The decision described the Teapot Dome lease to be the result of a conspiracy between Fall and Sinclair to defraud the United States:

> The negotiations were secret, and the lease made without competition; that responsible persons and corporations desiring to obtain lease were by Fall, in collusion with Sinclair, denied opportunity to become competitors of the Mammoth Company. . . . Fall and Sinclair conspired to defraud the government by making the lease without authority and in violation of law and to favor and prefer the Mammoth Company over others.[14]

The Court found that Secretary of the Navy Denby released his authority to Fall, and they offered as evidence a letter written by Fall that stated he wished to gain control of the oil. Fall wrote that his department would get the Navy reserves by an executive order, and that "if they meet with your approval and no changes occur to you, kindly return them . . . in order that the matter may be taken up with the President."[15]

While the civil trials were being argued, the first criminal trial opened on November 22, 1926, when Fall and Doheny appeared before the Supreme Court of the District of Columbia to answer the charge of conspiracy. Fall himself did not testify, although many of the Teapot Dome veterans such as Walsh, Daniels, Daugherty, and McLean appeared. In this trial, the jury acquitted (found not guilty) Fall and Doheny of conspiracy (a secret plan to commit a crime). The charges against the defendants were completely dropped. Sinclair also faced prosecution in another trial for contempt of the Senate, and he was found guilty. In yet another trial, Sinclair and Fall faced the Justices of the United States Supreme Court on charges of conspiracy. This time, Sinclair was sentenced to six months in jail for contempt of the Senate PLC.[16]

So far, the main player in the Teapot Dome scandal, Albert B. Fall, had avoided punishment. His bad health and low profile made him harder to prosecute, but new evidence was about to emerge in the second round of investigations.

chapter seven

RESULTS AND LESSONS LEARNED

MORE INVESTIGATING— Beginning in 1928, the Senate started a second round of investigations into the Teapot Dome scandal. This time, the Senate hearings were brief and not so dramatic. The second investigation began when Paul Anderson, a reporter for the St. Louis *Post-Dispatch*, wrote an article asking what had happened to the original $3 million "investment" Albert B. Fall had received from Edward L. Doheny.

Doheny owned the Pan-American Petroleum Company, and he set up the other company to shield his illegal activities. The "investment" was really a bribe that Fall had received from Doheny in order to get the Elk Hills oil field lease. The Supreme Court had already ruled that the fake company was organized "for no legitimate purpose."[1]

Second Investigation Urged

Anderson prompted Senator George W. Norris to ask for a new investigation into Teapot Dome. Norris, originally from Ohio, was known as a progressive who supported regulation of businesses and utilities. He helped pass the Tennessee Valley Authority Act in 1933. The act established government ownership of electric power plants along the Tennessee River.[2] Norris argued that the investigation should look into "all the illegal transactions connected with the fraudulent and dishonest sale . . . of the said naval oil reserves."[3]

Anderson had first approached Senator Thomas J. Walsh, who had been the leading investigator in the first investigation, and asked him to lead the second investigation. Walsh declined because he was tired of the publicity. The newspapers once again got involved in the controversy, writing articles about the huge sums of money paid to Albert B. Fall and diverted to the Republicans. But the second investigation never reached the emotional frenzy or sensationalism of the first investigation into Teapot Dome. By the time the second investigation ended in 1928, the oil industry had already taken steps toward change. It wanted to clean up its tarnished image. The second investigation failed to turn up any new evidence of dishonest dealings.

Fall Investigated Again

Albert B. Fall had faced serious accusations in his trial for accepting a bribe from Doheny. On October 7, 1929 (almost six years after the first investigation began), Fall limped into the District of Columbia Supreme Court leaning on a cane. Fall looked much older than his sixty-seven years. A nurse assisted him into a wheelchair and helped him to stand up when the judge entered the courtroom.[4] He looked worn out and frail. He collapsed to the floor during the first day of arguments when the government's prosecuting attorney completed his opening address to the jury. He suffered from a hemorrhage. Three court-appointed doctors stated that he was not healthy enough to appear in court. The prosecuting attorneys did not want to be seen as badgering a dying man, so they asked for a postponement. Against the advice of the doctors, Fall himself insisted that the trial go on and that he attend. Fall's attorney said that his client was entitled to "vindication before he passes into the Great Beyond."[5]

Prosecuting Attorney Owen Roberts worked hard to produce evidence of Fall's bribes. The defense concentrated on proving that Fall had been victimized, and that he played only a secondary role. At one point, the defense called Doheny to the stand. Like Fall, Edward L. Doheny was much older and in a weaker condition than during the peak of his oil tycoon days. Doheny explained in detail that he and Albert B. Fall had been friends for forty-three years.

Owen Roberts argued that Fall's physical condition was not the concern of the jury. Roberts got right to the point. "It is simple," he said.

> There are four things of a controlling nature for you to remember. One is that Doheny wanted the lease of the Elk Hills. The second is, Fall wanted money. The third is, Doheny got the lease, and the fourth is, Fall got the money . . . . The only drainage in this case was from Doheny's to Fall's pocket.[6]

Fall Found Guilty

The trial of Albert B. Fall for conspiracy ended on October 25, 1929, when the jury foreperson came in and announced the guilty verdict. Fall slumped in his chair and turned to look at his wife and daughter, who were crying. In consideration of his physical condition, Judge William Hitz sentenced Fall to one year in prison and fined him $100,000. The maximum penalty was three years and $300,000. Judge Hitz told Fall he would have handed down the maximum penalty were it not for Fall's frail health and the jury's recommendation of leniency (a lesser sentence). Since Fall suffered from tuberculosis, the judge allowed him to serve his term in the mild climate of his home state of New Mexico. Fall left the prison early after serving nine months and nineteen days of his sentence, most of it in the prison hospital in Sante Fe. He never paid his $100,000 fine. The many court trials of the scandal had depleted Fall's savings. He claimed he did not have any of the money from his dealings with the oil businessmen. He had also lost his ranch in New Mexico when the bank took it back for nonpayment of loans. In the words of a reporter, Fall had become "a pathetic, broken old man."[7]

Doheny and Sinclair Set Free

Although Fall served time in prison for accepting a bribe, another jury found Doheny (who had offered the bribe) not guilty. After a brief trial in the District of Columbia Supreme Court in 1930, Doheny was set free.

In yet another trial, Harry F. Sinclair of Mammoth Oil

Company fame was sentenced to six months after he hired a detective agency to follow the jury during his trial. Sinclair received the punishment due to contempt of court (of failure to follow normal rules and procedures). Later, Sinclair was acquitted of any conspiracy with Fall. In the end, of the many people involved in Teapot Dome, only Albert B. Fall actually served time in jail as punishment for criminal charges.

Teapot Dome's Legacy

Teapot Dome's legal history ended with the Fall, Doheny, and Sinclair verdicts, but the effects of the scandal would be felt for years to come. A fundamentally unhealthy relationship between big business and government had been exposed. As a result of the Doheny acquittal, Senator George W. Norris said, "It was impossible to convict a hundred million dollars in the United States."[8] The popular 1920s image of the businessman-tycoon as an American hero may have saved Doheny from a conviction. Historians still argue about whether Albert B. Fall was a scapegoat (a convenient target to direct blame away from wealthy businessmen like Sinclair and Doheny). Sinclair, Doheny, and others probably deserved more blame than they received. Albert B. Fall, on the other hand, deserved all the blame he received.

Perhaps the lessons of Teapot Dome can be found not in the guilt or innocence of any one person but in the need to change a bad system. The three biggest lessons of Teapot Dome are: (1) scandals in government are always present,

(2) politicians use scandals to advance their careers or destroy the careers of others, and (3) America lacks a sound policy for energy conservation.

In the 1920s, politicians were open to influence from greedy businessmen, and the government did not enforce or improve the oil industry's regulations. The biggest lessons learned were that the potential for scandal in government, the politicization of scandal, and the attempts by politicians (both Republican and Democrat) to capitalize on scandal were always present. Americans had grown used to the influence of huge corporations in Washington, D.C. The Sherman Antitrust Act of 1890 and the breakup of a dominant industrial giant in *Standard Oil Company* v. *United States* in 1911 gave people the impression that big business could be limited. However, one troubling lesson of Teapot Dome was that politicians could become rich through special favors given to them by the government and by industry.

Energy Policy Needed

Another lesson to come out of Teapot Dome was the fact that the United States lacked a sound energy policy. With all of the mad scrambling to get the oil out of the ground and make money, people forgot that as a fossil fuel the supply of oil is nonrenewable. The supply of oil will some day disappear, but nobody knows when. Yet another lesson of Teapot Dome is that America relies (even today) too heavily on oil to power the economy. Since all industries and transportation systems use petroleum products, the companies that drill, refine, and deliver oil have tremendous

One of the most important lessons of Teapot Dome is that America (even today) relies too heavily on oil to power its economy.

influence. The United States has had serious discussions about our reliance on oil, but we have never moved away from using it for heating homes, running factories and generators, and powering transportation.

How did the energy policy in the United States change after Teapot Dome? The three oil reserves originally set aside for the Navy for national defense purposes existed for more than eighty years. Saving oil in the ground for Navy ships made sense in the early twentieth century. Many of today's Navy submarines, battleships, and aircraft carriers now run on nuclear energy. Protecting our military interests does not seem to relate as closely to maintaining an oil supply today as it once did. The threat of a war with Japan or the Soviet Union, for example, seems remote. Japan does not have a large military and enjoys friendly relations with the United States. The former Soviet Union broke into independent republics after Mikhail Gorbachev tried to modernize the Communist nation.[9]

Government Versus Business

Teapot Dome's legacy does still show up in fundamental conflicts between the interests of government and business. Government is supposed to represent and protect the rights of people, while businesses exist to earn a profit and to pay the workers. Can government provide effective control over the oil business in the future? The Teapot Dome scandal proved that government did not have sufficient insight into the oil business in the 1920s.

The Great Depression began in 1929 after the stock

market crashed, and during the 1930s America tried to protect its oil markets from inexpensive imports. Many people lost their jobs and their life savings, businesses went bankrupt, and people forgot about the issues of regulation. In 1930, President Herbert Hoover signed into law the highest import tax in history, the Smoot-Hawley Tariff, designed to protect American oil producers from imported oil.[10]

When Franklin D. Roosevelt was elected in 1932, he proposed extensive new federal programs known as the New Deal.[11] These programs put people back to work through government-designed construction and conservation projects. Roosevelt did not change Hoover's policy of discouraging foreign oil imports. Roosevelt approved a bill in 1940 authorizing increased naval presence in both the Atlantic and Pacific oceans in response to the possibility of war. Realizing a bigger Navy would need more oil, Roosevelt appointed Secretary of the Interior Harold Ickes to serve as petroleum coordinator. President Roosevelt established the Petroleum Reserves Corporation to increase the government's involvement in the oil business during World War II.[12]

Inexpensive energy helped the amazing growth of the economy in the United States after World War II ended in 1945. The country expanded rapidly for most of the twentieth century without a federal energy policy. Americans did not see the need for a federal energy policy when oil was inexpensive and businesses were running efficiently.

A conflict arose when business leaders wanted to increase oil production while environmentalists wanted to restrict new drilling for oil. Oil tanker spills and new offshore oil drilling in wilderness areas upset environmental leaders in the 1960s and 1970s. Huge gas-guzzling cars, long drives to work, and houses heated by fuel oil represented how much Americans thrived on inexpensive oil. Nearly 10 percent of the world's oil production is burned up every day in the vehicles on American highways.

The 1970s Oil Crisis

A great shock came in the 1970s when the Organization of Petroleum Exporting Countries (OPEC) in the Middle East announced oil production cuts. The effect on the American economy was devastating as the price of gasoline jumped from 35 cents to 65 cents per gallon.[13] Americans panicked as long lines began to form at gas stations. People were afraid that they would not be able to buy gasoline to run their cars and trucks. Oil production in the United States had peaked in 1970 and declined after that. It was less expensive to buy oil from OPEC nations than to produce it in the United States. The oil crisis of the 1970s shows what happens with reliance on imported oil.

During the oil crisis of the 1970s when OPEC nations cut production, oil businesspeople approached Representative Edward Herbert, chairman of the House Armed Services Committee. At that time, the Armed Services Committee controlled the original three Navy oil fields of Teapot Dome, Elk Hills, and Buena Vista. Herbert told the oil businesspeople that when he had become chairman, he had pledged to his predecessor that he would never

Nearly 10 percent of the oil produced in the world is burned up every day in the vehicles on American highways.

lease the three fields to private companies. The previous chairperson had given the same pledge to the chairman before him, all the way back to the 1920s. The legacy of the pledge goes back to a congressman who had been very angry over Teapot Dome. He sponsored a law requiring a pledge to be handed down from chairperson to chairperson.[14] Herbert told the oil businessmen he did not consider the 1970s oil shortages to be serious enough to justify using the Navy oil fields.

In 1976, Congress created the Department of Energy (DOE) and shifted control of the Navy's petroleum reserves at Teapot Dome, Elk Hills, and Buena Vista to this new agency. The Elk Hills field, in which Chevron Oil Company holds a 22 percent interest, has been producing oil for years. In 1995, Congress debated selling the federal share of all three oil fields. The DOE estimated that the sale of Elk Hills alone could bring in $1.6 billion to help ease the federal budget deficit.[15] The much bigger problem, still not resolved today, however, is the reliance of the United States on non-renewable fossil fuels. Efforts to protect the environment and restrict pollution led to significant restrictions on new oil drilling and exploration. Congress created the Environmental Protection Agency (EPA) in 1970 to watch over industries. The Clean Air Act encouraged the move away from coal to cleaner-burning fuel oil and natural gas to generate electricity.

The death of President Warren G. Harding in 1923 touched off the Teapot Dome scandal. Many historians regard the scandal as evidence of Harding's inability to control his own Cabinet and effectively run the government. The story of the Harding administration "has been used in virtually every presidential election since 1924 as an example of evil and the epitome of a bankrupt 'do nothing' political philosophy."[16]

Harding served in office for 882 days. He accomplished some positive measures such as agricultural reform, debt reduction, and business assistance. While President Harding is chiefly remembered for the Teapot Dome scandal, the issues raised by the scandal have still not been resolved. Big businesses still have great influence in government. Government agencies such as the EPA and the DOE are not able to watch over all energy businesses. In addition, despite some efforts to develop solar, nuclear, and nonpolluting energy sources, the United States still relies too much on a dwindling oil supply for basic needs. Whether we will see another Teapot Dome scandal remains to be seen. In the meantime, Americans need to continue developing alternative energy sources and ways to conserve nonrenewable fossil fuels like oil, coal, and natural gas.

Questions for Discussion

1. Based on your reading of this book, do you think that Harding willfully allowed the oil reserves to be sold? Explain your answer.

2. Albert B. Fall, secretary of the Interior, believed that the oil should be pumped out of the ground and stored in tanks in case the Navy needed it during a time of war. Do you think Fall was right, or was he just trying to make money for himself?

3. How do current environmental laws affect the oil industry today? Find the name of one large oil corporation and do research in the library and on the Internet to learn about laws that affect drilling, refining, delivery, and preservation of oil.

4. In Chapter 5, Senator Walsh discovered the secret code telegrams being sent to President Coolidge. What reasons would Edward McLean have for sending secret telegrams? Why was this damaging to the Republican party?

5. Do you think Teapot Dome was the worst government scandal of all time? If so, why? If not, what scandal was the worst?

6. To what extent do you think the president should be active in issues of the environment and conservation of natural resources?

7. The Teapot Dome scandal was mostly about oil and the ability of businesses to make a fortune from selling oil with secret privileges given by government. How important was oil to the scandal? Could Teapot Dome have happened if it had involved alcohol, gold, or something else?

8. Do some research on the Republican presidents of the 1920s: Harding, Coolidge, and Hoover. Which president most successfully guided the country during difficult times? In your opinion, were these three presidents always trying to come out from under the shadow of Teapot Dome?

9. Write a short essay about the cultural life of America during the 1920s. Describe the music, clothing, lifestyle, standard of living, and hopes and dreams of the average American family living during this time. If you could travel in a time machine, would you like to visit the 1920s? Explain your answer.

Chapter Notes

Chapter 1. The Mysterious Death of President Harding

1. "President Harding Dies Suddenly," *The New York Times*, August 3, 1923, p. 1.

2. Ibid., p. 5.

3. Francis Russell, *The Shadow of Blooming Grove: Warren G. Harding in His Times* (New York: McGraw-Hill, 1968), p. 574.

4. Ibid., p. 575.

5. Ibid., pp. 575–576.

6. Ibid., p. 576.

7. Ibid., p. 619.

8. Ibid., p. 577.

9. John Mack Faragher, ed., *The American Heritage Encyclopedia of American History* (New York: Henry Holt, 1998), p. 762.

10. Russell, p. 582.

11. Ibid., p. 589.

12. Ibid., p. 591.

13. Robert K. Murray, *The Harding Era: Warren G. Harding and His Administration* (Minneapolis: University of Minnesota Press, 1969), p. 450.

14. William Allen White, *The Autobiography of William Allen White* (New York: Macmillan, 1946), p. 623.

15. Murray, p. 451.

16. Ibid.

17. "President Harding Dies Suddenly," p. 7.

Chapter 2. America in the Jazz Age

1. Ross Gregory, ed., *Modern America: 1914–1945* (New York: Facts on File, 1995), pp. 90, 127.

2. Jan Palmowski, ed., *Oxford Dictionary of Twentieth-Century World History* (New York: Oxford University Press, 1997), pp. 660–663.

3. Ibid., p. 374.

4. John Mack Faragher, ed., *The American Heritage Encyclopedia of American History* (New York: Henry Holt, 1998), p. 1029.

5. Kendrick A. Clements, *Woodrow Wilson: World Statesman* (Boston: Twayne Publishers, 1987), pp. 168–169.

6. Lois Gordon and Alan Gordon, *The Columbia Chronicles of American Life: 1910–1992* (New York: Columbia University Press, 1995), p. 97.

7. Palmowski, p. 637.

8. Faragher, p. 315.

9. Gordon, pp. 97–98.

10. Faragher, p. 1058.

11. Ibid.

12. Ibid., p. 902.

13. Ibid., p. 310.

14. Ibid., p. 815.

15. Geoffrey Perrett, *America in the Twenties: A History* (New York: Simon and Schuster, 1982), pp. 105–107.

16. Ibid., p. 107.

17. Arthur M. Schlesinger, Jr., *Running for President: The Candidates and Their Images, 1900–1992* (New York: Simon & Schuster, 1994), vol. 2, p. 107.

18. Ibid., p. 108.

19. Ibid., p. 110.

20. *Congressional Record*, 67th Congress, 1st Session, pp. 169–176.

21. Ibid., p. 170.

22. Robert K. Murray, *The Harding Era: Warren G. Harding and His Administration* (Minneapolis: University of Minnesota Press, 1969), p. 427.

23. M. R. Werner and John Starr, *Teapot Dome* (New York: Viking, 1959), p. 96.

24. Murray, p. 429.

25. Ibid., p. 430.

26. Francis Russell, *The Shadow of Blooming Grove: Warren G. Harding and His Times* (New York: McGraw-Hill, 1968), p. 569.

27. Murray, p. 433.

Chapter 3. Events Leading Up to Teapot Dome

1. J. Leonard Bates, *The Origins of Teapot Dome: Progressives, Parties, and Petroleum: 1909–1921* (Urbana, Ill.: University of Illinois Press, 1963), p. 236.

2. Bruce Bliven, "Tempest Over Teapot," *American Heritage*, August 1965, p. 105.

3. William Allen White, *The Autobiography of William Allen White* (New York: Macmillan, 1946), p. 623.

4. Carl Sferrazza Anthony, "Top 10 White House Scandals," *George*, January 1999, pp. 36–37.

5. Irwin F. Fredman, "The Presidential Follies," *American Heritage*, September/October 1987, p. 39.

6. Bliven, p. 21.

7. Ibid.

8. Richard N. Current, T. Harry Williams, and Frank Freidel, *American History: A Survey Since 1865*, 5th ed. (New York: Alfred A. Knopf, 1979), vol. 2, p. 624.

9. Burl Noggle, *Teapot Dome: Oil and Politics in the 1920s* (New York: W. W. Norton, 1965), pp. 56, 74.

10. Bliven, pp. 104–105.

11. Gary Libecap, "What Really Happened at Teapot Dome?" *Second Thoughts: Myths and Morals of U.S. Economic History* (New York: Oxford University Press, 1993), p. 157.

12. Noggle, p. 36.

13. Ibid., p. 15.

14. Ibid., p. 6.

15. Ibid., p. 7.

16. Bates, p. 239.

17. Noggle, p. 11.

18. M. R. Werner and John Starr, *Teapot Dome* (New York: Viking, 1959), p. 6.

19. Noggle, p. 13.

20. Ibid.

21. Werner and Starr, p. 6.

22. David H. Stratton, "Behind Teapot Dome: Some Personal Insights," *Business Historical Review* (Winter 1957), p. 386.

23. Bates, p. 227.

24. *The Encyclopedia Americana*, (Danbury, Conn.: Encyclopedia Americana, 1998), vol. 8, p. 483.

25. Bates, p. 228.

26. Ibid., p. 231.

27. Ibid., p. 232.

28. Ibid., p. 234.

29. Ibid., p. 237.

30. Werner and Starr, p. 5.

31. Bliven, p. 22.

32. Francis Russell, *The Shadow of Blooming Grove: Warren G. Harding and His Time* (New York: McGraw-Hill, 1968), p. 610.

33. Bliven, p. 22.

34. Noggle, p. 36.

35. Bliven, p. 101.

Chapter 4. Senate Hearings Force Out Albert B. Fall

1. Robert A. Divine, T. H. Breen, George M. Fredrickson, and R. Hal Williams, *America: Past and Present*, 4th ed. (New York: HarperCollins, 1995), pp. 703–704.

2. Burl Noggle, *Teapot Dome: Oil and Politics in the 1920s* (New York: W. W. Norton, 1965), p. 34.

3. Ibid., p. 35.

4. Ibid.

5. *Congressional Record*, 67th Congress, 2nd Session (April 15, 1922), pp. 5567–5568.

6. Ibid., p. 5792.

7. Ibid., p. 6042.

8. Noggle, p. 42.

9. "Harding Maintains His Stand," *The New York Times*, May 7, 1922, p. 1.

10. Geoffrey Perrett, *America in the Twenties: A History* (New York: Simon & Schuster, 1982), p. 184.

11. *Congressional Record*, 67th Congress, 2nd Session (May 13, 1922), p. 6893.

12. Divine, Breen, Fredrickson, and Williams, p. 705.

13. Noggle, pp. 51–52.

14. William Allen White, *The Autobiography of William Allen White* (New York: Macmillan, 1946), p. 621.

15. M.R. Werner and John Starr, *Teapot Dome* (New York: Viking Press, 1959), p. 110.

16. *Hearings Before the Committee on Public Lands and Surveys*, United States Senate, Senate Resolutions 282, 294, 434 (Washington, D.C.: Government Printing Office, 1924), p. 186.

17. Ibid., p. 188.

18. Ibid., p. 248.

19. "General Hines Charges Fraud and Waste," *The New York Times*, October 23, 1923, p. 9.

20. Werner and Starr, p. 159.

21. Noggle, p. 67.

22. "Denies Sinclair Gave to Democrats' Funds," *The New York Times*, January 27, 1924, p. 9.

23. Noggle, p. 74.

24. Ibid., p. 79.

25. "Coolidge, In Midnight Statement, Takes Up Oil Scandal," *The New York Times*, January 27, 1924, p. 1.

26. *Congressional Record*, 68th Congress, 1st Session (January 28, 1924), pp. 1537–1541.

Chapter 5. Teapot Dome Smears Its Next Victims

1. "Demand in Senate That Denby Quit," *The New York Times*, January 29, 1924, p. 1.

2. *Congressional Record*, 68th Congress, 1st Session (January 28, 1924), p. 1523.

3. Burl Noggle, *Teapot Dome: Oil and Politics in the 1920s* (New York: W. W. Norton, 1965), p. 97.

4. *Congressional Record*, 68th Congress, 1st Session (January 28, 1924), pp. 1518–1549.

5. "Demand in Senate That Denby Quit," pp. 1–2.

6. Noggle, p. 108.

7. "Coolidge Defies Senate on Denby," *The New York Times*, February 12, 1924, pp. 1–2.

8. Bruce Bliven, "Oil Driven Politics," *The New Republic*, February 13, 1924, pp. 302–303.

9. Arthur Schlesinger, Jr., Fred L. Israel, and David J. Frent, eds., *Running for President: The Candidates and Their Images*, (New York: Simon & Schuster, 1994), vol. 2, p. 781.

10. Noggle, p. 118.

11. *Congressional Record*, 68th Congress, 21st Session (February 29, 1924), pp. 3299, 3410.

12. "Daugherty Is Ousted By Coolidge," *The New York Times*, March 29, 1924, p. 1.

13. Ibid.

14. Noggle, p. 131.

15. *Congressional Record*, 68th Congress, 1st Session (March 18, 1924), p. 4406.

16. Noggle, p. 141.

17. "Daugherty Is Ousted By Coolidge," p. 1.

18. Donald R. McCoy, *Calvin Coolidge: The Quiet President* (New York: Macmillan, 1967), p. 220.

Chapter 6. Teapot Dome and the Election of 1924

1. Arthur Schlesinger, Jr., Fred L. Israel, and David J. Frent, eds., *Running for President: The Candidates and Their Images*, (New York: Simon & Schuster, 1994), vol. 2, p. 127.

2. Donald R. McCoy, *Calvin Coolidge: The Quiet President* (New York: Macmillan, 1967), p. 254.

3. Francis Russell, *The Shadow of Blooming Grove: Warren G. Harding and His Time* (New York: McGraw-Hill, 1968), p. 783.

4. Ibid., p. 782.

5. Ibid., p. 783.

6. Ibid., p. 131.

7. M. R. Werner and John Starr, *Teapot Dome* (New York: Viking, 1959), p. 195.

8. Burl Noggle, *Teapot Dome: Oil and Politics in the 1920s* (New York: W. W. Norton, 1965), p. 195.

9. Werner and Starr, p. 199.

10. Ibid., p. 200.

11. Noggle, p. 183.

12. Werner and Starr, p. 206.

13. Noggle, p. 183.

14. *Mammoth Oil Company* v. *United States*, 275 U.S. 13 (1927).

15. Ibid.

16. *Harry F. Sinclair* v. *United States*, 279 U.S. 263, 749 (1927, 1928).

Chapter 7. Results and Lessons Learned

1. Burl Noggle, *Teapot Dome: Oil and Politics in the 1920s* (New York: W.W. Norton, 1965), p. 97.

2. John Mack Faragher, ed., *The American Heritage Encyclopedia of American History* (New York: Henry Holt, 1998), p. 927.

3. *Congressional Record*, 70th Congress, 1st Session (January 9, 1928), pp. 934, 1185.

4. M. R. Werner and John Starr, *Teapot Dome* (New York: Viking, 1959), p. 281.

5. Francis Russell, *The Shadow of Blooming Grove: Warren G. Harding and His Time* (New York: McGraw-Hill, 1968), p. 637.

6. Werner and Starr, p. 283.

7. Noggle, p. 214.

8. Ibid., p. 211.

9. Francis Russell, p. 994.

10. Edward W. Chester, *United States Oil Policy and Diplomacy: A Twentieth Century Overview* (Westport, Conn.: Greenwood Press, 1983), p. 16.

11. Faragher, p. 804.

12. Chester, p. 20.

13. Divine, Breen, Fredrickson, and Williams, pp. 957–959.

14. Patrick Crow, "Teapot Dome's Legacy," *Oil and Gas Journal*, vol. 93, September 1995, p. 46.

15. Ibid.

16. Robert K. Murray, *The Harding Era: Warren G. Harding and His Administration* (Minneapolis: University of Minnesota Press, 1969), p. 533.

Glossary

bootleggers—People who illegally made alcohol during Prohibition.

bribe—To offer money in exchange for preferential treatment or special deals.

Department of the Interior—The government agency in charge of conserving natural resources in the United States.

Eighteenth Amendment—Addition to the Constitution in 1919 that made the manufacture, sale, or consumption of alcoholic beverages illegal.

Justice Department—The government agency responsible for the enforcement of laws.

Prohibition—The period in American history between 1919 and 1933 when alcohol was illegal or prohibited.

speakeasies—Secret clubs where people went to consume alcohol illegally during Prohibition.

Veterans Bureau—The government agency responsible for taking care of the needs of former members of the United States military.

Further Reading

Hargrove, Jim. *The Story of the Teapot Dome Scandal.* Danbury, Conn.: Childrens Press, 1989.

Joseph, Paul. *Warren G. Harding.* Minneapolis: ABDO Publishing Co., 1999.

Steins, Richard. *Taft, Wilson, Harding, and Coolidge: The Complete History of Our Presidents*, vol. 8. Vero Beach, Fla.: Rourke Corporation, 1997.

Traylor, Myrna E. *The Time-Life Student Library: Twentieth Century America.* Alexandria, Va.: Time-Life Books, 1999.

Yapp, Nick, ed. *The 1920s.* New York: Konemann, 1998.

Internet Addresses

Grolier Presents the American Presidency: Teapot Dome
<http://gi.grolier.com/presidents/ea/side/teapot.html>

Discovery School's A–Z History of Teapot Dome
<http://www.school.discovery.com/homeworkhelp/worldbook/atozhistory/t/549180.html>

The White House: Warren G. Harding
<http://www.whitehouse.gov/history/presidents/wh29.html>

Index